More Police on Patrol

by Linda Kleinschmidt

AJ Publishing, Hartford, Connecticut

Illustrations by Pepper Velez

Design and layout by Deena Quilty

Editing by Deena Quilty

More Police on Patrol

Published by AJ Publishing, PO Box 4277, Hartford, CT 06147-4277

First printing: March 1998
Second printing: June 1998

Visit AJ Publishing's Website at www.AJPublishing.com

Other related title: **Police on Patrol: The Other Side of the Story**

All in a Day's Work

This book is dedicated to all law enforcement officers, past, present and future.

ACKNOWLEDGMENT

I'd like to thank the hundreds of law enforcement officers from across the country for allowing me to interview them on a one-to-one basis, as well as those who submitted written responses through e-mail and snail mail and those who spoke with me over the phone and face-to-face. By nature and occupation, officers in general are very cautious and suspicious individuals. I am pleased the officers trusted me enough to speak very candidly, although it did take a considerable amount of time and effort on my part to gain that trust. The responding law enforcement personnel will see that I've treated them fairly and with the respect they deserve. Their confidence allows me to show the public what their daily activities entail.

I'd especially like to thank the departments which allowed me to ride with a number of patrolmen and patrolwomen on their shifts and see first hand what they encounter on a day-to-day basis. Also, I'd especially like to thank the department which allowed me to go out with their Vice & Narcotics officers on a drug bust and see what their job is like dealing with the drug community.

The support and encouragement I received from the law enforcement community was overwhelming. Thanks to everyone.

Special thanks to:

Connecticut Police Chiefs Association

Chief Robert E. Kosienski - Meriden, CT Police Department

Lieutenant Michael Manzi - Hartford, Connecticut Police Department

Corporal Robert L. Ward, Jr. - Upper Providence Township Police Department
Montgomery County, PA

and every other officer I interviewed.

Deena Quilty (design, layout and editing)

Deena Quilty, the principal of Quilty Communications, specializes in graphic design and marketing communications. After many years of corporate marketing experience, Ms. Quilty began the business in 1991 and continues to enjoy her work that combines the best of creativity and technology. Her company also produces advertisements, logo designs, catalogs, and electronic marketing materials, including web sites.

Pepper Velez (illustrations)

The talented illustrator for "More Police on Patrol" is a 15-year veteran of the Waterbury Connecticut Police Department. He is a professional illustrator with over 20 years of experience. His first love is drawing for comic books. Political satire is also a favorite which many who know of him and his work can attest to. Even though humor is his forte, he can also be seen doing "graffiti" style art. He has a great talent for capturing on paper what others can only imagine.

"ROLL CALL"

Prayer for Policeman ix

Introduction 1

Who Are We? (Author Unknown) 5

Excuses 9

      Motorist's Excuses 31

Routine Calls? 37

Accidents & Incidents 73

Sounding Board 100

Commentary 109

      Frustration – by anonymous Police Officer 110

      Me, The Lousy Cop – Author Unknown 114

      Code 2 – by Lieutenant Michael Manzi 116

      Let's Make It Personal – by Linda Kleinschmidt - 118

The Permanent Tribute (Connecticut Law Enforcement Memorial) 121

About the Author 124

A Prayer for Policemen

Oh my Lord, my God,
As I enter into my daily life as
a law enforcement officer,
I think of those which I am sworn to protect.
I cannot think of any selfish thing
pertaining to myself; only to give of myself
and to provide the safety
that I have given my word to provide.

Please give me strength and the wisdom that
are necessary in this, my profession; so that my
decisions are fair, decent and honest. Let me be
strong in my endeavors; guide me in this work I
have chosen, and watch over me so that I can do
your work another day. And if I should lose my life
protecting those I am sworn to protect, then please
make this a better place to live in because of it;
letting my loved ones and friends believe that my
life wasn't lost in vain.

Amen.

Written by Chief Robert E. Kosienski of the Meriden Connecticut Police Department for
the dedication of Connecticut's Law Enforcement Memorial, 1988.

X

INTRODUCTION

First of all, I am *not* a police officer, nor am I or have I ever been employed by any law enforcement agency at any time in my life. I've written **More Police on Patrol** for the same reason I wrote **Police on Patrol: The Other Side of the Story**, because I am tired of seeing the police get bad-mouthed by the media, criminals and the uninformed general population. The public has absolutely no idea what the men and women wearing the badge really do out there on the streets.

The original idea of writing these positive, real life situations that police encounter came from my friends in the Hartford Connecticut Police Department. A number of them used to share my morning newspaper for a few years. (It's always amazing how many people can share the same newspaper.) They would talk about seeing the same faces over and over again being arrested for a variety of crimes. The newspaper would have a story and very few, if any, facts regarding the cases. A distorted and highly publicized story about the police would also slant towards the alleged criminal. It's because of the lack of this truth in print that I decided to write my first book and now, this one.

It became apparent to me that the public's view and perception of a police officer is distorted, to say the least. The media in general is of little help in educating because their main interest is sensationalism and ratings, in order to satisfy their sponsors and advertisers.

This past summer, a local TV network affiliate had as their lead story—not a bank robbery and arrest of the captured suspects or the possible strike of the unionized correction officers—but, "Too many drunk driving stops: how they hurt local businesses." It appears that a particular municipal police department had stopped and arrested over 230 inebriated individuals for DUI in the course of the recent calendar year. In relation to their size in comparison to other law enforcement agencies in the area, this was a major accomplishment. But instead of the media praising the police officers for saving countless lives of innocent men, women and children from these drunkards driving home in their deadly weapons, they were persecuted. We saw the media interview local saloon owners who complained of a 75% drop in alcohol consumption, and we saw visibly intoxicated patrons who complained about how the police wait and follow them home. We were also privy to the sight of an actual stop of an inebriated man who had been driving himself home. We watched him stumbling as he walked the line, slurring as he spoke. The media turned this into a *bad* thing!

Introduction

There are a tremendous number of dedicated and caring individuals within our law enforcement communities, but as with any profession or job, there are a few people who should not be police officers. I did encounter a small handful of these maladjusted individuals, and it's because of them that I strive even harder to bring to light the positive aspects of those who proudly wear their uniforms.

More Police on Patrol is also written for the uninformed. My comments throughout the book are meant to make you think about your actions and reactions to those fine individuals who are sworn to protect the communities for which they service. If you were given a motor vehicle ticket, most likely you deserved it. And if you were arrested for beating your wife, child or other individual, you deserve to be locked up.

Unfortunately, the judicial system is set up to protect the criminals and make innocent victims always fear for themselves. It is the officers that are the ones who comfort those in times of anguish. They console those grieving citizens when they have to tell them that the local crack dealer shot and killed their son accidentally. The same drug dealer whom they've arrested no less than a dozen times and was allowed back on the street because the judge wanted to give them one more chance. Or because they served only six months of an eight year sentence, when someone decided that the jail was overcrowded. (This, for your information, is one of the biggest fallacies perpetuated by those in certain positions.)

We need to start asking the tough questions of those we've elected, such as "Why do we allow criminals to be placed back out on the streets after little or no time served?" We should be allowed to see in print or on television a picture of the criminal and their rap sheet, including the time served for each previous offense and the name of the judge who gave them that particular sentence. We should make it mandatory that five years equals five years, not seven months or less.

Crime is a universal problem. People need to get involved to stop it. They need to take responsibility for their own actions and stop putting the blame elsewhere. Children learn by example, and as I've observed, many people are setting some very bad examples for our younger generations.

Too many people are worried about the Constitutional rights of the criminals, at the expense of the taxpayers and the victims. Jail is meant to be a punishment. Often, it is not. It's up to each one of us to see that the criminals are held accountable for their crimes. A person who commits a crime should lose their rights, not *gain* more rights and privileges once behind bars.

It is my firm belief that those repeat offenders should be removed from society for as long as possible. The idea of having "a bad life" just doesn't cut it. Most of these leeches and parasites have no clue as to what it means to be an American, let alone a civilized person. They don't know what hard work is, or honor, or patriotism. The phrase "you owe me because…" is a bunch of garbage.

The only people I "owe" anything to are the forefathers of this country who left their origins to cross the Atlantic into the unknown and start a new life. A life which would offer freedom and free education. A life where if you worked hard, you could become anything you wanted to. They fought wars and lost their lives by the thousands for what they believed in: freedom and justice for all.

From the American Revolution and the Civil War, to World War I & II, Korea and Vietnam, and more recently the Gulf War, men and women with a sense of duty and patriotism have fought for and defended those freedoms which we hold so dear. So when I am told I owe someone because of his or her skin color or ethnic background, forgive me if I look like I'm about to lose my lunch. I find it hard to believe that anyone who tells me that would lift a finger to fight for our country or even knows what hard work really is. I owe you criminals and parasites – nothing.

The police are meant to serve and protect, but many times their work is wasted. They do their job and arrest those which are deemed guilty of a crime or breaking the law, yet we blame the officer if we see the criminal out on the street again the same afternoon. It's not the police, it's our legal system and laws. Give the officers a break. Help provide them with information so they can solve the crimes or apprehend the suspects. Don't think that someone else will get involved. *You* are that someone.

We can make a difference, if only to be informed. Just as this book will allow you to read about the funny, strange and sometimes tragic events and circumstances that our men and women in law enforcement encounter, it is meant to let you in on a world few civilians have ever thought about.

Even though I've focused on a number of humorous stories in this book, I am by no means trying to dismiss the negative side of police work. I have just decided to keep certain areas of this book lighthearted. In fact, just by bringing attention to the lighter side, the public will be able to gain a better understanding of the unpredictable nature of our communities.

Introduction

WHO ARE WE?

Author's note: The following "Who Are We?" was sent to me by e-mail and we were unable to track down the original author of the article. After consulting several police officers and having been given their opinion on the article, not only did they agree that it was something worth being printed in the book, but they also felt it should be placed in the front, and not with the other commentaries in the back of the book. Since I respect their views and totally agree with the contents of "Who Are We?," please read on.

We're the people that you may see every day and night. We're the people that you depend on one way or another. We're working for you 24 hours a day, 7 days a week 365 days a year.

When you and your children pass us in the store, and you can't control them, you make them afraid of us. You tell them if they don't behave, you'll tell us to "get them." My friend, we aren't monsters. We don't want them to be afraid of us. We want them to know that we're their friends, and they can trust us.

Do you know who we are?

Sometimes, we have to play the role of lawyers, judges, psychiatrists, reporters, medics, marriage counselors, investigators, firefighters, and many, many times, just be a good listener. These are just a few skills that we must be able to utilize at any moment in the performance of our job.

We're constantly scrutinized by the media, and you, the public. We're bashed by you. If one of us makes a mistake, it sometimes makes the local news, and possibly even national and world news.

Many of you are more interested in what a few of us do wrong than what most of us do right. You forget that we're not perfect. We're human, and we do make mistakes. Have you ever made a mistake?

We have the same emotions that you do. If something is funny, we laugh. If something is sad, we cry. When repeat offenders are released from prison and placed back into society to rape, rob and murder again, we get angry just like you. We also wonder why they are put back out.

Who Are We?

We suffer from the same problems that some of you do. Some of us at this very moment are thinking about committing suicide. Some of us already have. Some of us, if not most, have marital problems. Some are alcoholics, and yes, some of us even have problems with drugs. Again, we're just like you.

We're of every race, sex, religion, nationality and even sexual preference known to mankind, yet, if we strike back to defend ourselves, we're called racist and prejudiced.

Do you know who we are?

Most of you have no idea what we go through every day and night. You have no idea what kind of decisions we must make in a split second. Decisions that may forever change someone's life, family or future. Decisions that a jury will have hours or days to decide whether we were correct or not.

Many people would love to cause us pain, injury or even death. Some wish we didn't exist at all. We're cursed, ridiculed, shot at, cut, beaten, ambushed or murdered in cold blood by some. Would you ever imagine that we're here for those people also? Would you believe that we're the only thing that stands between you and them?

We see things that would horrify most of you. Things that you may think only exist in large cities. That's a common misconception. We see death, broken bones, dismembered bodies, and cut throats. The list is too long to really go on. These things are everywhere. A lot of things you see only on TV or at the movies are all too real to us.

We see innocent little children that have no choice but to live in dirty, smelly, roach-infested homes because their parents would rather sit on their butts and live on welfare in a government-funded housing complex than to go out and get a job. We see parents that would rather spend money getting high on drugs than on taking care of their children and raising them in a clean environment. Some of these parents are only children themselves.

As I said before, we're human, and we have feelings. It hurts knowing that these children may never get to see and do things that other children with loving, caring, hard-working parents are doing. I wonder if any of them will ever get to see that magical wonderland called Disney World.

Yet, our job is one that looks appealing to some of you. Especially when you see us stopped for lunch. We've heard some of you say things like, "I wish I had a job that would pay me to sit around and eat." Of course, you don't think that the very next minute we may be fighting for our lives, or yours.

When you see us riding down the road, and you, not knowing where we're going, or what we're about to face say, "I wish I could get paid to ride around all day and write tickets." My friend, I wish that was all we had to do.

Do you know who we are? I think you do.

You don't see us as we ride through your neighborhoods late at night, trying to protect you, your family and your property from the thieves who could care less about how long and hard you worked for everything you own. You may not know this, but they are roaming your neighborhood at night too, while you are fast asleep. They're looking for anything of value that is easy to get. Things that you carelessly leave unsecured or laying in your yard. No neighborhood is completely safe.

When something is taken from you, you call us. Some of you will complain and wonder where we were when your property was taken. The sad but true story is that we are extremely outnumbered by the bad guys. We can't be everywhere at once, and they know that. I wish there were more of us.

You should know who we are by now. If you don't, you will soon.

Now, the types of crime and the people that I have mentioned aren't the only ones that we come in contact with. We also come in contact with you, the citizen that never does any wrong. We're all too familiar with you and the remarks that you make when our paths meet for whatever reason. Whether it's running a stop sign, a red light, speeding, or DUI. If we had a dime for every time we heard you say, "I pay taxes! Why don't you leave me alone, and go get the drug dealer standing on the corner?" or "There are people out there doing worse than me!" or the famous . . . "I pay your salary!" we would be rich! We know that those of you that make an honest living do pay taxes. So do we!

Concentrate only on the drug dealers? How many innocent people would be injured or killed if we were to ignore the people that travel too fast, or the people who get behind the wheel while intoxicated? The number now is too high, and is still climbing.

I can't help but wonder how many lives we have saved by stopping the speeders and the drunks. Could one life have been yours, or one of your family members? We know there are people doing much worse than you, but the bottom line is, there are many laws that must be enforced, from minor traffic violations all the way to hard core crimes such as rape and murder.

Who Are We?

To remark, "I pay your salary," all I can say is, "Well, we're doing our job, boss."

If for some reason you still don't know who we are, we're the Police Officers, Sheriffs Deputies, State Troopers, State Police, FBI, and everything in between. We are many, but are still too few!

As I said at the beginning, we are always here for you. If you need us, call. Even if you don't, you don't have to be afraid of us. Remember that we are on your side. You can talk to us anytime you see us on the side of the road, in a parking lot, or walking in a store. If some of you would just get to know us, I think you would find out what I've tried to explain. That is, we are just like you ... we just have a different job.

EXCUSES

I'm sure a number of you have been on the receiving end of a ticket or at the very least, a verbal reprimand or written warning. How many times have you heard someone complain about getting a speeding ticket or other motor vehicle violation and then express resentment towards the officer issuing them a ticket? This is a rhetorical question because I've heard the complaints, and I've been a culprit too. "How dare they stop me when everybody else does it? and "Who does he think he is, sitting out of sight? They should be required to show themselves so we can slow down instead of get a ticket," are just a few comments I've heard.

For those of you who have encountered your local or state's "finest," what's the first thing you thought or said to yourself when you looked in your mirror and spied those unmistakable flashing lights? For a few of you profanity comes to mind, not necessarily out loud, but the thought was there. Next, those neurons start firing at a rapid pace, as you're pulling to the side of the road, attempting to come up with an answer to the officer's impending question or stern statement: "Do you realize you ran that stop sign?" "… made an illegal turn?" "… were exceeding the posted speed limit?"

Undoubtedly your heart rate has increased and you've quite possibly broken out in a cold sweat, either from the thought of receiving a ticket or the fact that your insurance rates are on the rise. But most probably from the brain activity overload of coming up with "the excuse." Granted, there are a few of you who actually politely take the ticket and apologize for breaking the law. For those of you, I commend you on your honesty.

"What can I tell the officer, which he or she will possibly believe and will influence the officer's decision in my favor?" is the typical reaction. Something sympathetic, like a health-related excuse either about yourself or concerning someone you just left or were thinking about going to see? Usually you need to play it by ear. Or maybe the "urgent" excuse. For this one you need to be able to use your body language and readily have available to you the ability to exaggerate facial expressions. The "funny" excuse can come in handy if you're the nervous type or very chatty. The full use of hands and a few slaps on your own forehead will usually give you an edge.

Ultimately, we all try to come up with a way to justify our flawed driving habits, but somehow if our "excuse" doesn't work after we've expended an excessive amount of energy coming up with the explanation we thought would be our salvation and are then given a ticket, then we have a propensity to blame the officer. It wasn't him or her who had their foot on our accelerator, or didn't put pressure on the brake. We did—or didn't. They may have had to match or exceed our speed in order to get us to pull over, but it was us who broke the law first. So before you ignore another motor vehicle code, either come up with a foolproof excuse (I'm still searching for one) or think about the consequences. But one thing you should not do is blame the officer for your stupidity or dumb luck on being stopped. They are just doing what we pay them to do: their jobs!

Here are some interesting excuses which were given to sheriffs, police officers and other related law enforcement officials across the country. A few actually worked and the recipients only received a verbal or written warning from the understanding officer. Some of the other violators weren't as fortunate.

At the end of this chapter is a subsection containing a few excuses that were told to me by civilians and their encounters with the men and women in blue.

Early one morning during rush hour, I pulled a woman over for driving erratically; she was swerving back and forth across the solid line. Her excuse: "I was straightening my pantyhose, officer."

The guy pleaded with us not to give him a ticket for speeding. He'd borrowed the car in question without permission and wanted to get it back before the owner found out it was missing.

A woman I'd pulled over for running a red light had her adolescent grandson in the car with her. The mature woman told me she didn't know why I'd stopped her. When I mentioned that she'd gone through the red light, she remarked incredulously, "I did?" Her grandson then chimed in "Grandma, you said, 'Oops' as we went through the light." Out of the mouths of babes.

"My wife just phoned me at work and she's ovulating. We're really trying to have a child and I'm hurrying home to try and get her pregnant."

"I was speeding officer because my wife just called me on my car phone to let me know that our dog was dying. I just wanted to be there at his side."

The man said he had just picked up his car at the auto shop when I'd stopped him for speeding. He said he was just testing to make sure the car was fixed properly. I asked him if it was. He said, "Yes" and asked if I was still going to give him a ticket. I did and I told him to look on the bright side, "At least your car runs well." He wasn't amused. Incidentally, the garage he mentioned that had done the repairs on his vehicle was over ten miles back.

One afternoon I stopped a local woman for speeding and weaving in and out of traffic; she had her teenage daughter with her at the time. I inquired as to why she felt it necessary to drive so recklessly. The woman told me, "I was speeding, officer, because I'm running late. It's my daughter's first day of driving instruction and I wanted to get her there on time."

I was doing a routine seat belt enforcement stop, when I observed a young female drive past without her safety harness in place. I waved her over and approached the window. She then began to cry hysterically. I questioned her as to what her problem was and between sobs indicated she had just come from the vet's office where she had her sick cat, "Fluffy" put to sleep. She was distraught. Now, being pulled over by me had "pushed her over the edge." I told her I had intended on giving her a written warning. Suddenly she perked up and said, "Oh, O. K." and her cat was a lost memory. Realizing it was the "crying trick," I then told her that she ought to be an actress and her award was a ticket. Now I saw real tears. Incidentally, she later admitted to not even owning a feline.

The woman couldn't understand why I'd pulled her over. I asked for her license and registration. I indicated to her that the registration tag was not up to par. She readily admitted that she'd used India ink and made her own expiration sticker for the plate. What she'd failed to realize is that it had rained the night before and the ink ran. Oops...

When I approached the window of the automobile, I could see the woman's hair was a little tousled and that a bottle of ibuprofen was on the front seat. She explained why she was speeding: "Officer, the cramps from my period are so bad that I have to scrunch up while I'm driving and I guess while doing so, I must have pushed down just a little too much on the gas pedal."

A motorist traveling in excess of 80 mph passed me on a residential street early one evening. Her excuse was that she was the leading lady for a play being performed across town at the theater. She expressed that she had to get there quickly because she was the "headliner." I lectured her that the way she was driving, she could become a headline in the newspaper on the obituary page. I gave her a ticket but had her follow me to the theater.

At three in the morning I stopped a young woman driving a VW down a local street. She was completely nude. I inquired as to why she wasn't wearing anything and why she was out at this time of the morning. She said she couldn't sleep and decided to take a dip in the ocean and had forgotten her towel at home. Instead of getting her nightgown wet, she thought she'd "air" dry.

I stopped a man for exceeding the posted speed limit. His excuse, "I'm rushing to the hospital to give a blood transfusion to my wife who gave birth ... yesterday." He was a little late.

We frequently get calls from people in the local neighborhoods complaining about the speeders and the people running residential stop signs. One morning while sitting in someone's driveway near a stop sign, a woman didn't even slow down. She went straight through it, without stopping. On top of that, I clocked her on radar doing 47 in the 30 mph zone. When I pulled her over she became belligerent, saying, "You can't give me a ticket. I'm the one who called the station about the problem with the other people who don't live on this street." We get all kinds.

"I've got a kidney infection and I drank about a gallon of water. I really needed to use a restroom, so I'm hurrying home."

"My wife was brought into the hospital and is at this very moment giving birth. I'm supposed to be there to, as she put it, 'Get out what I put in her almost nine months ago.' That's why I'm driving like a madman, officer."

"It's not my fault for speeding, officer. Gravity keeps pushing my foot down on the gas pedal."

The man was furious when I put my lights on and had him pull over. He said that there was no way that I could prove that he was speed-ing. I told him that I clearly got him on radar doing 73 mph. He said it was impossible. I asked, curiously, "Why?" He then indicated that he needed to get something from the trunk of his car. I became more than apprehensive when he pulled out his tire iron. Just as I was about to ask him to calmly put down his "weapon," he went to his passenger rear tire and popped off the hub cap. "That's why," he said while pointing at the aluminum foil balls that had spilled from behind the hub cap, onto the roadside. I told him that I still wasn't quite sure what he was talking about. He then enlightened me. Apparently, it is his belief that the aluminum foil blocks the rays from the radar gun which is therefore unable to get a reading. He also added that all four tires had the aluminum foil, so at any angle that the radar gun was aimed, it would be unsuccessful at clocking the vehicle. I assured him that I did in fact catch him on radar. He then suppositioned that maybe because he bought the store brand and not the name brand aluminum foil, that there was a difference in the quality of the product. I then wrote out his ticket as he pondered the possibility of low quality aluminum foil being his downfall.

───────────────

One sunny spring afternoon, we were doing seat belt enforcement in our patrol area when we stopped a woman who was not wearing her safety harness. She stated she had no intention of wearing her belt because she'd recently had breast surgery and no longer needed to keep her breasts from jiggling while she drove her car. I thought that the seat belt was for safety, not to reduce breast jiggle!

───────────────

The woman's excuse for exceeding the speed limit was rather unique; she said she was part Indian and "the winds told her to speed." She was also drunk.

───────────────

"Officer, I was speeding because I just got the car washed and didn't want to have water spots."

I stopped this young woman for crossing the center line several times while driving on a major thoroughfare. She was wearing very dark sunglasses. When she handed me her license the picture didn't appear to match her face. Then again, with the glasses on, I couldn't really tell. I asked her to please remove the glasses and also inquired as to why she was unable to hold her lane. Before she answered, I had my explanation. The pupils of her eyes were as big as quarters. Talk about scary looking. She'd just been to the eye doctor's and her eyes were still dilated. I asked her not to drive for at least an hour so her eyes could get back to normal, and then I would just give her a verbal warning.

———————————————

This guy driving a truck went flying past me while I was running radar, just outside the city limits. When I finally caught up to him and pulled him over, he said he was "…looking for a gas station. I didn't want to run out." I mentioned to him that he must have past at least three gas station while I was pursuing him. He responded, "Oh, I know. But the gas stations here are three cents more per gallon than the one near my house. That's where I'm headed."

———————————————

The big difference between stopping men and women that use the excuse of "running out of gas and speeding to a gas station," is that the women forget to turn off the engine when I'm writing their ticket.

———————————————

I was doing about ten mph over the speed limit when another motorist passed me like I was standing still. I turned on my lights and siren, got right up behind him and motioned for him to pull over. He not only kept going, but sped up. He was doing close to 90 mph and refused to pull over. I radioed for back up and several moments later, the other officer pulled up next to him with his lights and sirens going and pointed to the side of the road. The driver then obliged and pulled to the side of the roadway. When we got to the window, he appeared stunned. "What did I do wrong, officers?" was his question. I asked him why he didn't pull over eight miles back when I first came upon him. He said he didn't know that the lights were meant for him to pull over. Unbelievable.

We administered a sobriety test to the intoxicated driver after we stopped him from driving down the center line on Main Street. Upon taking the test, he said to us, "This test is too hard. I couldn't do it if I were sober."

I pulled a woman over early one Sunday morning for speeding and weaving across the center line. The older woman apologized because she wasn't paying attention to her driving. She was busy saying her rosary while driving and wanted to finish before she got to church. She indicated she was already running a little late.

I pulled a guy over driving a "muscle car" for doing 63 in a 40 mph zone. He said he was unaware that he'd broken the posted limit, because his speedometer was disconnected. He was planning on selling the car and didn't want the person buying the vehicle to know the real mileage.

We stopped a priest driving an older model car doing 15 mph in a 45-mph zone. His excuse for driving so slow was that he wanted to finish saying his rosary before he arrived at the local hospital to visit with several of his parishioners.

The guy I stopped for running the stop sign gave me an honest answer. "If I knew you were sitting there, I would have stopped, honest." Well, if he had stopped, I told him, "I wouldn't be giving you this ticket, honest."

A young teenager passed me, driving an old beat-up Chevy truck like I was standing still. He was polite but a little on the cocky side. He indicated that he frequently speeds because every once in awhile he just gets this burst of adrenaline and needs to drive fast. Considering the fine that the ticket amounted to, I asked the young man if he had a part time job after school. He said that he did. I told him that the next time he felt that burst of adrenaline coming on, think about how many hours he'd have to work in order to pay off the fine. He got very quiet and said he hadn't thought about it that way. I suggested that if he had that much energy, joining a sport would be a lot better than the possibility of killing himself or other innocent people with his driving. He agreed.

I stopped a man for speeding and he told me that during the morning and evening rush hours I couldn't issue him a ticket for speeding. I asked him why, and he responded, "Because, those are the 'free' hours for motorists." He said he was surprised that I wasn't informed of this law. His father taught him that years ago. I issued the ticket and told him to get his "free" rush hour from his father.

While running radar at the base of a long winding hill, I clocked a man doing close to 90 mph. When I asked him why he was going so fast, he said that he frequently throws the car into neutral whenever he goes down a hill or grade in order to save gas. He said he doesn't bother braking unless he goes too fast for comfort. I told him that I didn't see any brake lights until I turned my lights on. He said, "Yeah, I know."

During rush hour, I spotted a motorist, driving in the breakdown lane of the three-lane highway doing an excessive amount of speed in comparison to the rest of the weary drivers. I was able to catch up to him and pull him over. He said he was in a rush to bring home the ice cream cake that he had on the front passenger seat before it melted. He didn't want to turn on his air conditioning because he wanted to save his gas. That's why he was driving fast on a busy highway. He thought that I'd understand. I told him I didn't and proceeded to issue him several citations.

I stopped a young man for doing 75 mph in a 55 mph zone, shortly after morning rush hour. I advised him that I was citing him for speeding and he said he knew he was exceeding the limit by a lot. He indicated that he was late for a hearing at the court. I asked if it was for speeding and he said, "No, for driving with a suspended license." I went back to the cruiser and ran a quick check on this gentleman. Not only was the young man very late for his hearing, but he was also given a ticket for speeding, for driving while his license was under suspension, and he received the bonus of having his car towed, too.

When I stopped the late model vehicle for speeding, I found the driver to be a man in his late 40's, slightly over weight and perspiring profusely. I asked him, "What's the rush, sir?" He said while shaking his head, "I'm running late for my doctor's appointment. I'm going there to have a stress test done."

When I stopped the teenager for driving down a one-way street, I received the usual stupid response. "I'm only going one way!"

I stopped a motorist for taking a right turn on red where it was posted "No Turn on Red." The motorist told me, "Officer, I looked everywhere for a sign that said not to turn right on red and I didn't see any sign." I indicated that if he looked at the traffic light there was one hanging next to it and there also was one on the side of the road indicating that there was no right on red. He said he didn't look at either of those spots that I'd brought his attention to.

When I walked up to the vehicle I'd just signaled to pull over, the window was down and the smell of hot pizza was in the air. Before I could say anything, the occupant of the vehicle started complaining about the pizza place not delivering. "If they delivered, I wouldn't have to be driving so fast to get home before the pizza gets cold. It's the pizza place's fault I was speeding."

The woman said she was speeding because she had bought her little kitty some treats at the new pet store. She was excited about seeing the kitty try her new "chewies," and that's why she was speeding.

I stopped this guy around midnight for speeding and asked him why he was in such a hurry. He responded that his license was going to expire soon and he wanted to get home before it did.

The slender young executive said that he was rushing home because his puppy had recently peed on the new drapes. His wife got angry and insisted that he buy her new drapes. He didn't know anything about purchasing drapes, so he'd hired a professional who was on their way over to his house as we were speaking. The drape man had said he could only make it there at a specific time and was not willing to wait for more than 15 minutes. If he was late, the drape man would be gone, he would have to get rid of either his dog or wife—he wasn't sure which one—because that's the ultimatum his wife had given him. So, he said, he was just trying to keep the peace in his small family and that's why he was speeding. I just gave him a warning. I felt bad for the guy.

The woman asked me not to give her a ticket for speeding. She had what she called a very good reason for exceeding the posted limit. She was on her way to court to fight the other speeding ticket she'd received recently and she was running just "a tad late." She also felt that my giving her another ticket would hurt her case, because she was sure she'd have to tell the judge why she was tardy.

As I approached the nicely dressed woman I stopped for speeding, I saw she was holding a melting ice cream cone in her left hand. A few drips landed on the door frame as she stuck her hand with the cone out the window. She asked me to hold it as she reached for her purse. I suggested that she take a few licks first, because it was melting. She said, "Oh, no thank you. I don't eat ice cream. I bought that for my husband and I was trying to get home before it melted completely. That's why you caught me going so fast."

I stopped this young female driving a small standard shift compact car for speeding on the highway. I indicated that she was doing 72 mph and the posted limit was 50 mph in that particular area. She looked at me wide-eyed and said while she put the brake on and threw the car into neutral, "Listen to this." She then revved the engine. "Officer, see, my little car can't go that fast." She revved the engine a second time. This time she gave it a little more gas. "It just couldn't have been my little car that you caught on radar." I decided to just give her a warning. I just wasn't in the mood to try and match wits with someone that didn't appear to possess any to begin with.

I was following a gentleman doing the speed limit, when all of a sudden he hit the gas and accelerated to 20 mph over the limit. I was about to turn my lights on when, just as quickly, he slowed down. I decided to give him a break and not stop him. A few minutes later he did the same thing. I turned on my lights and pulled him over. I inquired as to why he was making such radical changes in his speed. He responded while holding a cellular phone, "I'm not on digital yet, so I keep losing the reception on my car phone. I needed to get closer to the next tower to get rid of the static."

On my way back to the station one early spring day, I was following a young woman in a red sedan traveling at a reasonable speed. She had her driver's window down and she stuck her arm out as if signaling to make a left run. I immediately slowed down, but noticed that she didn't. A few moments later, she pulled her arm back into the vehicle. About two miles or so down the road, she did it again. I once again slowed down to give her proper distance while she made her turn and supposed that she had been mistaken earlier. Once again, she didn't turn, and quickly pulled her arm back inside the car. Finally, on her third attempt at motioning to turn and then negating the idea, I put on my lights and pulled her over. When I approached the window, she appeared perplexed. Being slightly annoyed, I inquired as to where she was going and why she kept using her hand signals for a left turn and then changing her mind. Her response, "I'm sorry officer, I wasn't attempting to make any turns. I'm on my way to work and I wanted to dry my wet finger nail polish before I got there."

When I stopped this well dressed man for DUI, I inquired as to why he felt the need to drive while intoxicated. He responded with slurred speech. "Because, occiffer, I'm too drunk to walk home."

While routinely patrolling my area, I noticed a car ahead of me accelerating to a high rate of speed, and then immediately slow down without the brakes lights coming on. As I approached, the driver made this peculiar maneuver again, while crossing the center line. I immediately used my siren and lights. Expecting to find the driver intoxicated, I was surprised to see a completely sober individual in the driver's seat. Before I could even ask a question, the driver of the vehicle offered an explanation as to his erratic behavior. "You're probably wondering why I crossed the line. Officer, my foot itched so much that I kicked off my shoe and was using the gas pedal to scratch it."

We caught a man stealing money from the parking meter. He said he hadn't used up all his time on the meter and wanted a refund.

This young pregnant woman went past me like I was sitting still. When I pulled her over, she let out a yell and then started her breathing techniques. She regained her composure and I inquired as to where she was headed because the county hospital was three blocks in the opposite direction. She indicated they were having a one-day sale on baby furniture at a local store and she thought she would have enough time to get there and purchase the bassinet she had seen been eyeing in recent weeks. Well, she never made it. She had the baby ten minutes after we got her to the hospital. When the husband arrived, we let him know about the baby furniture sale and he ran out to get the bassinet for his wife and new baby girl.

The young businessman was driving a small compact car when I pulled him over for doing 20 mph over the speed limit. He said that he still had the cruise control on that he'd been using while driving on the highway earlier, and said he was sorry. I'm somewhat familiar with that particular make and model of the car he was driving and told him that I didn't realize it came with equipped from the factory with cruise control. He admitted it didn't and that he was referring to his foot as the cruise control. Nice try.

This middle-aged woman went through a red light and took a left hand turn across a two-lane highway. When I pulled her over, she said that she didn't see a sign that said she couldn't take a left on red after stop. So she did. I told her the law says she can take a right on red after stop, but never a left. She thought it was both; she'd been doing it for years.

I finally caught up with the teenager who'd been driving recklessly, among numerous other motor vehicle violations, and asked for his license and registration. After confirming that his registration was expired, his license was suspended and he had no insurance, I asked him to step out of the vehicle. He stumbled out of the car and proceeded to fail the DUI test. I called for back-up and as we were placing him in the cruiser, he asked which three charges or tickets he was going to get. I told him that he had about a dozen different infractions in addition to the registration, license and DUI charges. He was under the impression that we could only give out a maximum of three tickets per motor vehicle stop and that he was able to choose which three. Incidentally, ignorance is not a defense in the court of law.

I stopped a man for speeding. The posted limit was 70 mph. He said he'd seen the sign and thought that 70 mph was the *minimum* speed.

I was doing radar in plain sight of the oncoming traffic when this female driving a red Volvo station wagon flew past me. I pointed to her to pull over, and she ignored my gesture and kept going. I got into the cruiser and caught up with her. She finally pulled over. I asked her what her hurry was and why she didn't stop. She said that the cable TV guy was coming to add another cable box at her residence and they gave her a four-hour window of when they were going to show up. If she wasn't there to wait for the cable person, she'd have to wait another week and a half. I only gave her a written warning for speeding and a stern talking to about not obeying an officer's request to stop. I could sympathize with her because I know how inconvenient it is when you're not given an exact time or hour when the cable people will arrive.

The woman pumped her own gas, then left, waving to the gas station owner, without paying. The owner got the make, model and plate number off the vehicle. When I arrived at the residence of the car's owner, I saw the woman in question getting back into her automobile. I stopped her and told her that she'd been accused of stealing gas from the station across town. She said that she didn't steal the gas; she'd forgotten her debit card and had to run home and get it. She said she waved to the guy at the station and yelled that she'd be right back. I told her that she'd better come with me to the gas station and explain it to the owner. Fortunately for her, he didn't press charges and she paid for the gas. She gave new meaning to the phrase, "Pump now, pay later."

I stopped the guy for speeding and gave him a ticket which resulted in a rather large fine. The man was pleasant to me, but I still had to issue the ticket since he was speeding in a school zone. As I started to walk away the man asked me what portion of the ticket was considered a donation, because he planned on writing it off on his taxes next April. I suggested that he'd better talk to his accountant before he attempted to do that, because none of the fine is considered a "donation" as far as I knew.

The station wagon with a family in it went speeding past me even though I (and my radar) was in plain sight. I thought it rather odd, but he actually looked like he sped up once he saw me. When I caught up to him, he readily pulled over. I could see and hear as I approached that the female front-seat passenger was yelling at him. "See, I told you we'd be late going to my mother's house. I told you to hurry up. Now you're getting a ticket for speeding. Boy, do you deserve it." I could see the two children, a teenage boy and younger girl sitting quietly in the back seat, as their mother complained. The man already had his license and registration ready by the time I got to his window. He asked if he could please get out of the car; I told him he could. He looked frazzled. Meanwhile, the wife was still yelling at him and now, me too. "Give him a ticket. That'll teach him to listen to me." I went with the husband to the back of the car and faced my cruiser behind it. He said, "Officer, I intentionally sped up so you'd pull me over. I couldn't take listening to her yakking any more. She never shuts up. I just needed a real human being to speak to and I saw you. I figured it was worth getting a ticket so I could have a few minutes of quiet without listening to her." He asked me to please take my time writing the ticket. I felt real bad for the guy. I only heard her for a minute or so and I already needed some aspirin. I told him I wouldn't give him a ticket. He thanked me and asked if he had to leave. I asked him what he thought of last night's basketball game and he smiled. We chatted for about ten minutes and I wished him a better afternoon.

I stopped this young guy for doing 55 in a 25-mph zone. When I got to his window he told me not to bother writing him a ticket. He had already received one ten minutes earlier from the officer across town. The guy thought that you could only get one ticket per day for speeding and he was now exempt from receiving addition citations. Wrong.

I stopped a middle-aged couple for running a stop sign late one afternoon. The guy politely asked me to hurry up and write the ticket because he and his wife were headed out to dinner. I mentioned that they had a lot of time because it was still rather early, about 4:15 or so, and I was sure the restaurant would still be open when they got there. The guy said the coupons they were using were for $2.00 off each meal if they were seated before 4:30 and the place was still five minutes away. I asked the guy to think about this: he'd save $4.00 on the meal, but the ticket I had to issue him for speeding was for $60.00. Seems like a financial loss to me, not to mention the accident he could have caused. He said he hadn't thought about it that way.

Motorist's Excuses: Stories from Motorists Themselves

Author's Note: It never ceases to amaze me how people will try just about anything to get out of a ticket.

While out doing book signings at a number of book stores, I took the opportunity to question people as to what excuse or reason they used to in order to get out of a ticket. The following excuses were told to me by individuals who had actually given these responses to police officers after they'd been stopped for a breaking the law. I found that young females between the ages of 17 and 22 were more likely to use sex or implied sex to try to get out of tickets. They were also more likely to file false reports by making up fictitious people who had made them scared or threatened them, causing them to speed or drive recklessly. What's even scarier is the fact that they would come up with very explicit details describing the vehicle and suspects in question. When I asked what would they do if there really was a person in the same area at the same time driving a vehicle similar to the one they'd just described, well, not one of them had ever taken the time to think about those consequences and the effects on other people. They were only interested in themselves.

Middle-aged men were more likely just to bitch about being caught. Trying to come up with some technicality on why they shouldn't have been given the ticket, these individuals were most likely to draw me a sketch to show the distance from the stop sign or where the officer had parked their vehicle while running radar. They just wanted me to validate that they were right and the officer was wrong. I would ask them if they were really speeding or really did run the light, and each time there was an admission of guilt. I'd tell them that the laws are there and the officer is just doing his or her job. I'd also have to stress upon them that I am not a police officer and that I've gotten tickets in the past, just like them.

Women between the ages of 40 and 60 were the ones most likely to complain about the lack of follow-through by their police departments in apprehending what they felt was the most under-addressed problem facing their communities: people speeding and running stop signs within residential areas. These are the ones that made me chuckle to myself, not out of disrespect, but because the police departments frequently do address this problem. The results are usually that the ones they stop are the people that live within the area that they received the complaints from. Also, on more than one occasion, it's been the original person who made the complaint that gets nabbed for running the stop sign or speeding.

Here are a few of the responses.

When the officer stopped me for speeding, I told him that it was impossible for my rusty piece of sh** to even go that fast. He said he was surprised that it did, but was nice enough to only give me a warning.

One day while I was driving down Interstate 95 from Boston to New York, I was stopped by a Connecticut State Trooper. I had a cooler on the front seat of my car and was cranking down the highway when I saw the flashing lights. I thought fast and came up with this bizarre excuse: "Officer, I just came from Bradley International Airport and I'm on my way to the Bronx Zoo. I just picked up this elephant sperm which had been flown into the wrong airport. If I don't get it there soon, it's going to expire and it would be a real shame to have wasted the elephant's sperm." I still can't believe the officer believed me and let me go with only a warning. [LK: I told him that the officer didn't believe him; it's just that he probably couldn't believe that you had the nerve to tell him that excuse.]

I told the officer that I was speeding in order to catch up to the car in front of me that was driving erratically. I was going to use my car phone to call in their license plate to the police as soon as I could read it.

I told the officer that just before that time of the month I get real horny and was on my way home from work early to have sex with my husband before he had to leave on a business trip that evening. He said he liked my priorities and let me go with just a warning. (I'm not even married.)

I got stopped for passing the school bus in a "no passing" zone. I had just wanted to get home before my kids got off the bus. It wasn't a good idea for me to pass the bus. Not only did I get a ticket for that, I got one for speeding and my kids saw the officer pull me over.

I got pulled over while driving my convertible Corvette for speeding. I told the officer that I needed to get my hair dried before I got home. My boyfriend hadn't wanted me to go to the beach for a swim because we had company coming over. I figured if I drove fast he'd never know the difference. Well, he did, especially since his mother saw me speaking with the officer.

I was cruising down the highway when I noticed the lights behind me. I just told the officer that one of my favorite songs was playing on the radio and it just made me drive fast. He knew the song and said that particular song had the same affect on him. He only gave me a warning.

I just told the officer the truth. I was exceeding the speed limit. I shouldn't have been and he agreed. He said that because I told him the truth, he'd only give me a warning.

I explained to the officer that I'd just gotten back from England after an extended stay and they drive 80–100 mph on their roadways. He didn't buy it. He said they drive on the opposite side of the road too. And that I seemed to have adjusted well to driving on the proper side of the highway, but the ticket would help to remind me that I was now back in the United States and I needed to obey the speed limits. Boy, that was a hefty fine.

A bunch of us guys told the officer we had just seen a Jeep driven by four females, all of which were topless. We were trying to catch up to them and see if we could get their phone numbers. Just as the cop started to say we'd have to come up with a better excuse, he hears over his radio a report of topless women driving down Main Street in a Jeep. He let us go. We never did get their numbers.

I was home on leave from the military when an officer pulled me over for speeding. He seemed at first to be slightly annoyed at the fact that I kept using the word, "sir." Out of habit when he asked me to get out of the car, I said, "Yes, sir" and then proceeded to stand at military parade rest. All of a sudden he eased up on his attitude with me. He thought I was trying to patronize him by responding with the phrase, "Yes, sir." He then asked what branch of the military I was in and we chatted for a few minutes. He said that once he saw me stand outside the car, he new that I was legit. He still gave me a ticket, though. Hey, he was just doing his job.

I had just left a rugby game where we'd won and one of the guys had tossed a beer at me. I missed catching the can and it exploded on my clothes. I didn't even have a sip of it. I left immediately because I had to go home and get ready for an evening wedding I was attending. I was running quite late and as my luck would have it, I was stopped by a cop for speeding. I'd forgotten about the beer which had sprayed on my sweats. That is, until the officer had me get out of my truck and walk the white line. He believed me about the beer spilling, but still gave me a ticket for speeding.

Excuses

ROUTINE CALLS?

This chapter deals with different calls and incidents that were either witnessed by the officers, or that they were summoned to investigate.

The stories in "Routine Calls?" encompass a very broad spectrum in order to show that the police encounter many different and unusual situations. Unlike what a majority of people believe, they don't just stop people for speeding and DUI. Law enforcement officers witness so much when they're out on patrol that most people would simply be astonished.

There is a lot more that occurs within your county and city limits than you could ever imagine. Don't think for even a minute that you know everything that goes on just because you read the newspaper or use your free time to listen to police channels.

Consequently, in defense of police who may not have been overly cordial to you, the officer usually has a very personal reason for acting aloof. When you get upset at a police officer for issuing you a ticket because you didn't have your child in a car seat, you may feel put out. What you probably don't realize is that the officer may just have come from arresting a man for sexually assaulting a 14-month old baby who's now in intensive care in the local hospital. And there you are speeding without your kid in a car seat. The officer may have just come from a serious car accident where people may have been killed or maimed for life. Your speeding or reckless driving may seem trivial to you, but what an officer witnesses daily are often tragic consequences. There are an enormous amount of variables that we as regular citizens fail to take into account.

There is a definite mix of different calls that are presented in this chapter. They're given very simply, and sometimes without the gruesome details. It's up to you, the reader, to use your imagination where I have left off. Some of these are funny, some tragic, and some will have you scratching your head, wondering whether there really are people out there completely lacking in common sense. (There are!)

Routine Calls?

A mother of three called to report a raccoon in her basement with a bottle stuck on its head. The animal was very difficult to trap. I finally got the animal into a burlap sack and then struggled to remove the partly shattered glass jar. The children were crying and the woman was very upset for the animal. I told her I planned on putting it out of its misery. The woman asked me to please bring it to the vet and I told her I would as long as she assumed responsibility for the bill. Immediately she changed her attitude and said, "Shoot it."

A masked man robbed a local convenience store. As he went out the door, he pulled off his mask. To his amazement, a girl he knew from his high school days was sitting in a car out front. He ran over to her and said, "You didn't see me here," then sprinted around the corner. He was so impatient to find out if she'd squealed on him, he went to the police station and pretended to need directions to a local street. We came around the front counter and handcuffed him.

A known felon decided to rob a beauty salon early one morning by first gaining access through the front plate glass window. He tossed a brick through the window and quickly jumped inside. We had no trouble apprehending him because he was so severely cut from the glass that he was lying in a pool of his own blood and was unable to move.

We were on a foot chase, catching up to a drug addict who'd just robbed the local convenience store, when after about five minutes we overcame him rather easily. He'd gotten so scared while fleeing with us in pursuit he pulled down his pants and had to take a sh**. Right in the middle of the path we were following him on.

We got dispatched to a local mall because of a young man shopping in one of the stores. He wasn't stealing anything, he was just shopping in the nude.

This particular felon was so brazen that after he robbed the local hardware store, he walked past the officer on traffic duty and said, "hello," while carrying a bag of stolen merchandise. The officer had already been radioed a description of the fleeing robber and quickly apprehended him. He was quite surprised at being arrested.

I was hired for an extra job to conduct traffic outside a residential home where the occupants were having a lavish party. One guest, driving a sports car, pulled up to me, got out, handed me the keys and headed for the door. I called to him and he said to park it anywhere. He thought I was a "Valet Parking" attendant. Hmmph. No tip.

We had a rash of auto break-ins in a relatively quiet neighborhood, and had beefed up patrol in the area. While patrolling, I noticed a car whose door was left ajar and decided to investigate. After a closer look on foot, I could see that several cars near each other also had their doors left ajar. I looked in a few autos and noticed their radios were missing, too. I radioed in for back up and we quietly started looking in cars in the immediate vicinity. To our great surprise, we found the crook inside a late model car, sound asleep, still holding a pillowcase full of the stolen radios. Needless to say, he was arrested.

A drunk man came home around 5:30 in the morning and realized he'd forgotten his keys. He broke a small pane in the front window to gain access to his residence. Once inside, he made himself comfortable on the couch after finding the remote and turning on the TV. Moments later a man came down the stairs and opened the front door for the police. The inebriated man had broken into his neighbor's house, not his.

One night while I was working a private job patrolling the parking area at a local night club, I observed two guys removing a battery from a vehicle. When asked if there was a problem with starting the car, they both said yes and that they were taking the battery to a gas station to be recharged. I asked if they were sure it wouldn't start. They insisted it wouldn't. I said, "Well, it started fine for me earlier when I drove it here." They were stealing the battery out of *my* car!

While patrolling my area late one night in an industrial zone, I observed two men unloading wood at one of the manufacturing companies by tossing the wood over the fence to a third guy. I stopped and spoke with them briefly to find out why they were tossing it over and not driving through the gate near the night watchman. They had indicated he wasn't there when they'd arrived and were in a hurry to off-load the 2' x 8's. I then left and turned the corner. Immediately I pulled the patrol car over, and radioed for back-up. When we quietly snuck up on them, we observed that they

41

were now loading up the truck with the wood, tossing it back over the fence, and *not* unloading as I was told earlier. I can always count on my instincts.

At the local train station, someone had left a briefcase on the platform. It had no outside identification and the conductor had reason to be concerned; that's why we were summoned. The briefcase was making a funny ticking noise. All safety precautions were taken by the bomb squad in determining the nature of the noise. The site was evacuated and to our relief, we found it wasn't a bomb, but a sex toy which had been accidentally turned on. We then called the owner (whose name was inside the briefcase) and asked him to come and retrieve his infamous briefcase.

Sometimes the stupidity of carjackers is amazing. This particular person decided to carjack a woman at knifepoint as she was getting into her car at a local cable television station. She was able to get away and ran back into the studio screaming for assistance. To everyone's disbelief, when they got out into the parking lot, not only was her car still there, but so was the carjacker. He was trying to drive her standard shift car when he had no idea of how to shift. He could only drive automatics. (This was also in a state which recently passed a law saying deadly force could be used against a carjacker.)

Years ago I stopped this drunk driver on a local road. I went to his window, got his license and registration and told him to stay put. No sooner had I gotten back into my patrol car, than he was at my window asking me—with intoxicating breath—what the problem was. I told him to just get back into his car and wait for me to come back. He got into his vehicle and closed the door. When I approached he was all upset. He told me through the rolled down window that he wanted to report a theft. Someone had stolen his "steering wheel, pedals and radio, but left the sound." I calmed him down as I helped him out of the back seat of his car and into my vehicle.

A man attempted to rob a local convenience store while wearing a trench coat and threatening the cashier with a bulge under his coat that he implied was a shotgun. When we apprehended the man shortly after he had left the store, we could only charge him with attempted robbery because the clerk didn't hand over anything when he demanded that she do so. The reason was that he didn't really have a gun under his coat, he had a Dustbuster and he didn't cover it up all the way.

One evening at the end of my shift, just as I was heading back to the station, I spotted a young woman driving a car with one headlight out. I pulled her over just to let her know about it. I'd had a very long day and didn't plan on writing any more tickets. I approached the window and this relatively attractive woman with blonde hair was sitting in the driver's seat. She asked what the problem was and I told her that a headlight was out, to which she responded, "Oh, really? Which one? Front or back?" I quietly walked back to my car and left.

A local man was obsessed with the notion that his neighbors were eavesdropping on his private conversations within the walls of his own home. So he put aluminum foil all over the roof of his two-story colonial house so his neighbors couldn't listen in anymore.

We have people bringing in all kinds of lost animals like cats and dogs, and asking us what to do about them. This one afternoon we had a citizen bring a baby calf into the foyer of the police department. Just as we were about to ask where they'd found the animal, it lifts its tail and poops. That wouldn't have been so bad except for the timing. The Chief was walking by, talking with another officer and didn't see the "accident." He slipped and fell right in the fresh fertilizer. We all bit our tongues and didn't laugh. As much as we wanted to, we didn't. At least not when he could hear us.

We were radioed a call about a break-in at a duplex residence. The owner of the apartment was home at the time. We knocked on the door, identified ourselves and entered the dwelling. It was awful. The place was trashed. I wondered silently to myself, what would make people do something like this to someone else's belongings. Garbage on the floor. Stuffing ripped out of the furniture and something gooey was stuck on the television set. Just then my partner turns and says to me, "She said it was the tenants upstairs on the second floor that had the break-in, not this apartment."

A number of years ago, during the 1960's, we had some of the peculiar people you heard about that dwelled in some of the rural towns across the country. One recluse called the department to report the theft of three two-cent bottles she was missing from the 200 or so she had kept on her shelf in the living room. Another time, she called to report bristles missing from her broom. These calls usually came during the lunar cycle when the moon was full.

A nude man on PCP was walking around a parking lot in broad daylight wearing only a pair of sneakers and a smile. We opened the trunk of the cruiser to get a giant plastic bag to put over him to cover his exposed private parts. He immediately hopped in the trunk of the car and closed himself in. We needed to call for assistance because he'd grabbed the keys as he jumped in.

A rather deranged man called 911 because he believed his neighbors were trying to poison him by pumping toxins into the pipes in his toilet.

The rather disheveled woman could always be seen walking around the city wearing a tinfoil hat. She said she felt it would protect her from the aliens.

A man called the police department to inform us that his dog had decided to commit suicide by hanging himself. The dog had fallen off the porch during the night and had used his leather leash as the means to do himself in.

Recently we had a rash of break-ins where the suspect would take the homeowner's portable phone and make calls to a 1-900 sex line. Once the batteries wore down, he would break into another residence and steal only their portable phones. In one instance, cash left on the table wasn't touched by the intruder and only the cellular phone was taken.

A rather eccentric, elderly gentleman complained to the police that he heard music coming from his toilet bowl. We suggested that it was probably the Tidy Bowl man and was completely harmless. He agreed.

People call 911 for the most ridiculous reasons. We've had calls from people asking the day of the week … calling to ask the time of day… and even people asking for the bus schedule.

A man was protesting the stench in the neighborhood. He decided that since he wasn't getting any action from the town, to load up his truck with chicken manure and park it in front of city hall. We had to use gas masks to approach the truck. There wasn't anything in the ordinances saying he was breaking the law. The only recourse we felt we had was to issue him a parking ticket once his two hours expired on the meter. He adamantly refused to move his truck. We then decided, for health reasons, to get a machine to suck the chicken manure out of his vehicle. The man later brought us to court, wanting his chicken manure returned to him.

I responded to an emergency call of a woman giving birth at a residence in the city's project area. I was able to respond quickly because I was in the vicinity; I arrived before the medical team. This rather large, unmarried female, living with her parents told me she was ". . . just . . . so surprised." I asked, "Because the baby came out so fast?" She responded while shaking her head, "No. I didn't even know that I was pregnant. I went to the bathroom because I thought I had gas, and this baby pops out! I was just. . . so surprised!"

We received a 911 call from a local residence. The dispatch had extreme difficulty in understanding what the female was saying; the woman's voice was muffled. Fearing the worse, like maybe an intruder had broken in and she was calling while hidden in a closet or under a bed, several cruisers were sent to the house. When we approached the front door, it opened before we even knocked. Standing in front of us was the home owner, holding an electric egg beater that had gotten wrapped around her tongue when she licked the cake batter and the mixer became engaged. No wonder we couldn't understand a word she was saying.

Routine Calls?

There's an ordinance in the city that you have to shovel the snow off the sidewalks in front of your building. On one particularly busy street, several juveniles decided to construct a number of large snowmen right on the sidewalk in the path of pedestrians, causing them to have to walk in the roadway to get around the obstructions. We spoke to the teenagers and asked them to remove their sculptures; they agreed. We thanked them and left the vicinity. We came back through the area about an hour later, only to discover four additional snow figures that were now adorning the walkway. They apologized and said they would dismantle them and reconstruct them on the vacant lot, down the street. We once again thanked them for abiding by the law. The next time we came through, we saw they had removed all of the snow figures except for one very large figure. The teenagers were nowhere in sight; so we decided the quickest way to remove the obstruction was to pull the cruiser up on that area of the sidewalk and knock it over with the car. When we hit the snowman, we came to an abrupt stop. The sculptors had built the snowman around a fire hydrant and freezing cold water was now spraying our vehicle and the surrounding area. It ended up being one of those days.

We received a call from a number of local residents telling us that they'd just seen a plane land at an abandoned airport. We went to the airport to find the two-seater plane on the runway and the pilot coming out of the woods. He indicated he knew the airport was closed, but he had to use the bathroom really bad and knew he wouldn't be able to get to an operating airport. I guess sometimes when you have to go, you have to go.

We were called to a residential home in an affluent area by the male owner of the house, because of a "peeping tom" in a tree outside his house wearing nothing from the waist down. We easily apprehended the "peeping tom" who'd tried to run away while putting on his pants and falling a few times in the wet snow. I spoke with the home owner while my partner stayed with the suspect. The father said that he looked out his son's bedroom window and saw the man looking in, and handling his private parts to the point of self-gratification. What upset the father even more was that the man was his son's Little League coach. It took all we could to keep the man from attacking the coach. The mother/wife then took me aside and said that there was a little bit of a misunderstanding. The coach was not peering in on her son. She was having an affair with the coach and she was in her bedroom, which is next to her son's bedroom, standing naked since she'd just gotten out of the shower. The coach would peer in the window on days that her son was still awake and her husband wasn't home. Tonight, her husband had come home early and saw the man in the tree and called police. Boy, I'll tell you, when the husband was told what was really going on, we had to call paramedics and a doctor to calm him down. What a mess!

While patrolling late one evening, we came across a vehicle parked in a cul-de-sac with the driver sitting in the driver's seat. His headlights were off and we went over to inquire as to why he was sitting in the dark. When we approached the window, we saw the man was clad in a red negligee and white stockings. Very large sized high heels were on the seat next to him. He was alone. He had no explanation or excuse, except that he felt like sitting in the dark in his car, wearing this particular apparel. We checked is I.D. and ran his plate. There was nothing unusual . . . except the guy.

Routine Calls?

I stopped a man in a busy parking lot for repeatedly spinning his back tires. There was the odor of burnt rubber and a lot of smoke coming from the tires. He told me that he usually doesn't "balance" his tires in a public parking lot, but he forgot to do it at home that morning and thought it best to do it as soon as he remembered. The man was under the impression that in order to "balance" his tires, burning off the tread was the way to do it. I told him that maybe he ought to go to a mechanic and have them explain to him the proper way to balance tires. Curiously, I asked him how often he bought tires during a typical year and he said that he replaced them every three or four months with brand new tires. Boy, his tire man must love having him as a frequent customer.

We were involved in what must have been one of the slowest police chases in history; the suspect was an elderly gentleman doing 20 mph on a major highway. He crossed over state lines and we now had to involve the state police of the bordering state. The man just kept moving. He wouldn't stop for our lights or sirens. He just hung onto the wheel with both hands and had his chin resting on it. We finally had to resort to a rolling road block: one vehicle gets in front of the auto and the others box him in, slowing down to a stop. When we finally got him to pull over, he was quite surprised to see all of us around him. He was in his 80's, blind in one eye and had cataracts in the other. He said he'd decided to take a ride on the highway because his license had just been renewed by the state via mail. He figured that if the state thought he was able to have a valid driver's license, then regardless of what his relatives and doctors said, "By golly, I'm going to exercise my right to drive."

A woman wearing a very conservative suit handed me her driver's license and registration as I'd requested for her failure to stop for the red traffic light. She was polite, so I decided once I got to my car to not write the ticket. I would just give her a written warning, instead of a ticket. When I walked back to the car, the woman had her blouse unbuttoned to her waist revealing a lace bra. I excused myself, walked back to the cruiser and wrote out a ticket instead of just the written warning. It's her loss for trying to use her body to get me to forget about a ticket.

Late one Friday afternoon, I pulled a man over for speeding. Immediately the woman in the car following pulled in front of the man's vehicle on the shoulder of the road. I first approached the man. When I got to his window and looked inside, the man had on a dress shirt and tie, and a briefcase sitting on his lap. He was nude from the waist down. I asked him where the rest of his clothes were and he pointed to the woman in the car in front of him. "She has them officer." I then glanced at the passenger seat and said, "I suppose the skirt and woman's thong underwear belong to her?" He nodded. I then asked for the female's garments, walked to her vehicle, and handed them in the window. She put his clothes into my outreached hand, and I proceeded back to the man who was now leaning his head on the steering wheel. He looked up and said, "Officer, I can explain, really..." I'd had a long day and decided that I really didn't want to know. I gave him a verbal warning for speeding and told him to keep his clothes on while driving a motor vehicle. I then walked to the woman's car; she was now dressed. She kept her head down as I spoke. "Embarrassing isn't it?" She nodded. I then went back to my cruiser and left.

My partner and I responded to a call at a local elderly housing apartment house concerning a man that was hallucinating. In talking to the retired gentleman we found that he truly believed that ghosts were coming out of the walls. I went out to the cruiser and retrieved a can of disinfectant spray. I told him it was actually anti-ghost spray and I misted the area where he believed the ghosts were most prevalent. He seemed satisfied that the repellent had done its job. Approximately a week later, the senior contacted our department and asked my supervisor where he could purchase a can of the anti-ghost spray so he wouldn't have to disturb us anymore. I had a little explaining to do.

This arrogant tuxedo-clad man double-parked outside a theater on opening night. He said he couldn't find a parking space and didn't want to have to park too far away, like the rest of the theater patrons. He then proceeded to tell me to "Hurry it up!" while I wrote the ticket. As fate would have it, I had to immediately direct traffic for the next 20 minutes while the obnoxious man sat in his luxury car and waited.

Around three in the morning, I stopped a young, scantily-clad female driving a sports car—on a relatively busy thoroughfare—for speeding and not stopping for a red light. She indicated that she was a dancer at a local strip club and was on her way home from work. She didn't think that she needed to obey the laws at that time of night. I told her that because she was doing an excessive amount of speed, I would have to write her a ticket. I went back to the cruiser and started copying the information off of her driver's license. I looked up to see her tossing what few clothes she was wearing out her driver side window. I immediately called for back-up. There was no way that I was going to approach the woman now without a witness. Today, people are so sue-happy, you have to always cover your backside. She was quite surprised when the other officer, a woman, showed up. The officer came to my window first and I got out, walking next to her, towards the naked motorist. My female colleague then picked up the woman's clothes, asked her to please redress herself "pronto," otherwise she would be charged with a variety of other offenses. Also, she indicated that once she was decent, I would then approach and give her the tickets. The stripper quickly put her clothes back on.

We were called to the security office of a major department store. The man in custody wasn't shoplifting, which is the reason why we usually end up at the store. The middle-aged man was found in the dressing room of the intimate apparel department using his hand to sexually gratify himself while wearing several different lingerie articles.

An angry woman came into the police department and demanded that the man who had sold her a rock of cocaine be arrested, because she said it looked like just a piece of hard baking soda. She felt she'd been ripped off; she'd paid for crack. We had one of the narcotics officers test it and found it was really cocaine. She seemed to calm down; that is until we arrested her for possession of an illegal substance.

We get some of the strangest medical calls. You wouldn't believe the types of objects that people insert into the different orifices on their person and then proceed to get them stuck. Everything from large coke bottles to even live creatures, like mice and gerbils. It kind of turns your stomach.

I approached a car in a secluded area which was known to be a spot for couples parking. I knocked on the window; the female was engaged in oral sex with her male companion. She looked at me, mouth still on the appendage, and motioned with one finger, as if to say "In a minute." I knocked on the window again and she repeated the gesture. Finally, she looked up and swallowed. She told me she had to finish what she had started.

We arrested the drug dealer after we'd gotten a call from a local dry cleaner's employee. The suspect had come by and dropped off his laundry bag as he usually did every week, except this time he dropped off a stash of drugs instead of his dirty clothes. He'd grabbed the wrong bag.

This guy had a fetish for ladies underwear: his neighbor's. We arrested him after he was found to have stolen over 100 pairs of panties over a number of years from his female neighbor. She knew that she was buying a lot of underwear, but had no clue as to where they were going.

On my way to work, I saw a man with a disabled vehicle. He had the hood of the late model Buick up and was looking at the engine when I stopped to help. Knowing a bit about mechanics, I easily got the car started and the man thanked me profusely. He even waved as he drove off. I then got to the station and was still in time for line-up. As I was heading out to my cruiser, we received a report of a stolen vehicle, meeting the description of the car that I had helped to start. I went back inside and the owners of the vehicle, an elderly couple, said they'd had a problem with their car and had walked to a nearby garage. They'd only been gone 20 minutes or so and when they got back with the mechanic, their car was gone. I told my supervisor, out of earshot of the victims, that I had a great eye-witness concerning the auto theft. They radioed out the description of the man and car along with the direction I saw him headed. Luckily, we were able to get the guy within a few minutes. Talk about feeling stupid. I actually helped a criminal steal a car, without knowing it of course.

We are frequently on the look-out for illegal aliens and drug traffickers, being so close to the Mexican border. Sometimes they use innovative ideas on how to smuggle drugs into our country. One time, they had put the illegal drugs inside a propane gas truck's tank and even had working valves. Their downfall was incorrectly spelling the name of the gas company on the outside of the tanker.

The 911 system is constantly abused by people with non-emergency related calls. For instance, we received a call from a woman who had told her children she was calling the police to have them arrested for not eating their breakfast. It's people like this that make children afraid of the police.

Routine Calls?

When we arrived at a "domestic," the man apologized to us for having to come out to his residence. He indicated that he had just snapped. He said he had become exasperated coming home from a hard day's work for the past thirty or so days to find that his wife had made mashed potatoes for dinner, again. That particular day when he had come home, she wasn't around. His dinner, including mashed potatoes was on the table waiting for him. He then proceeded to put the mashed spuds into all his wife's coat and shirt pockets. When his spouse arrived home a short time later with his birthday cake and placed it on the table, he said the cake just reminded him of mashed potatoes. He picked up the cake and threw it in his wife's face. That's how the fight started.

We were dispatched to investigate an alarm which had gone off at the local elementary school. When we arrived we didn't see any vehicles except for the janitor's, who was standing outside the facility, waiting for us. Once we entered the building and turned a corner near the gymnasium, we were dive-bombed by a flying object—a large bat. After we determined that there was no one else in the building, we had the task of securing the bat, because bats and small children do not make a great mix. We spent several hours trying to catch him, to no avail. We then tried everything we could think of to get him out of the building. Our success came just as the sun was about to rise, when we were able to finally get him out a window near one of the science rooms, by using the lid off a garbage can as a shield and a broom to swoosh him out into the early dawn air. We were relieved to have kept the bat from frightening the small children which would be arriving shortly. Unfortunately, we later found out that we had swooshed their science project to freedom.

We arrived at the scene of a domestic dispute to find the husband sitting out on the back porch of the duplex house, eating his dinner of fried chicken. The wife greeted us at the door wearing a dress which had been splattered with food: mashed potatoes, gravy and some other vegetables. Her hair was mussed and black mascara was smeared under her red swollen, tear-stained eyes. We informed her that we'd received a call from a neighbor of a disturbance coming from this residence. The wife then started talking non-stop, repeating herself and not really listening to our questions. We were able to decipher that her husband had tossed her around a bit and was now sitting outside. The husband's account of what happened was that he'd come home from work at the local steel mill. He had a tough day and just wanted some peace and quiet. His wife started complaining and nagging him from the moment he walked into the apartment to the time she put dinner on the table. He fixed his plate and went to go outside when she stood up and told him to stay there at the table because she wanted to talk to him. He said he did not care to listen and she stood in his way. He then put his plate on the counter and physically picked up his petite wife and placed her on the table on top of the food and other condiments, as well as the dishes. She screamed, and that's probably why the neighbor called. He then went outside to eat his dinner in peace until we showed up. She corroborated his story and said he did not hit her but he did pick her up and place her in the middle of the table. We still had to take an action, and he was arrested for breach of peace. We let him wrap up his dinner and take it with him to the station.

We were summoned to a local trendy restaurant because of several patrons who had come to the establishment earlier for dinner. We were informed by the owner of the restaurant that the patrons had been a little affectionate when they first entered and he thought that, for some people, that's wonderful. He had called us now because their affection had gotten out of hand. He said he made an attempt to get their attention, but was too embarrassed to lift the tablecloth and demand they get out. That's why he called us. There, in the back of the restaurant, all we could see sticking out from under the tablecloth—which fortunately went down close to the floor—were two sets of feet: one wearing black socks and the other with pink toenails and no footwear. The couple had decided to become intimate right there in the restaurant. When we were finally able to get their attention and have them get dressed, their only explanation was that their burning desire for each other took command of their senses.

Sometimes the criminals literally come to us. While demonstrating to children in a city neighborhood how the computer tracking system works from the cruiser's computer, another inquisitive individual began asking questions. He was asked if he had some form of identification on him for the demonstration. After his name was run on the computer, he was immediately arrested. He had a warrant out for his participation in an armed robbery several years earlier.

The only word for the guy is "scumbag." He robbed the young girl's lemonade stand of all the money she'd earned and was apprehended several days later after he'd stolen the purse of a woman in her 80's.

One Thanksgiving a few years ago, we responded to a domestic disturbance. Apparently the husband fed the turkey to his dog and the couple got into a massive argument which included breaking several pieces of furniture and a number of glass objects. The woman wanted the man arrested for feeding the turkey to the dog.

The guy, wearing only a pair of underwear, broke into a residence, assaulted the home owner, then fled. He'd left his wallet and shorts on the front lawn, so it didn't take long to identify and capture him.

A local guy robbed a bank while wearing a mask. He demanded that the cashier put money into the briefcase he'd brought with him. The bank robber then fled in a stolen vehicle. A short time later we found the vehicle, abandoned. Inside the vehicle was the briefcase, empty except for a business card tucked in the inside flap. The card ended up belonging to the bank robber. When questioned about the robbery, he admitted holding up the bank.

Sometimes the criminals aren't very bright. We had this guy walk into a local market and demand all the money the cashier had in her register. She complied and he fled the premises with the cash. The only thing he forgot was his wallet which he'd left on the counter. We easily apprehended the man at his residence a short time later.

We had a call one evening of a missing officer. Out on patrol, the officer had seen an open door at a local auto repair facility. He investigated. Upon entering the building, he fell into a grease pit and couldn't get himself out. When dispatch was unable to raise him on the radio, we went in search of him. When we found our colleague, he was rather upset, as well as slimy. But not as distressed as the other officer who'd lent him his brand new jacket.

Routine Calls?

We received a 911 call from a local drug addict wanting us to arrest the drug dealer he'd just made a "buy" from. He felt the cocaine he'd purchased was of poor quality and wanted the man to either replace it with better quality or get him his money back for him.

Over the past dozen or so years that I've worked the mounted patrol, I've seen my share of funny things that people do. Once in awhile my horse is the cause for the commotion. This one time I stopped a suspicious vehicle at a stop sign and asked the occupant for his license and registration. Just as he went to hand me his registration, my horse grabbed it and ate it. We both just watched in amazement. I was at a loss for words.

We had a report of a local convenience store having just been robbed. A description of the pick-up truck used as a getaway vehicle had just been radioed out to my partner and me. We were heading out of the mall parking lot when we saw a truck—matching the description of the suspect's—parked across several spaces with the headlights off but the engine still running. We immediately called for back-up and surrounded the vehicle and its occupants. Upon approaching the window, we could see that the male and female in the truck were stunned by our presence. In less than a minute, we were able to eliminate these two as suspects. He was so drunk, there's no way he could have held up the mini market. He couldn't speak clearly or even stand up. We brought him and his companion back to the station and had them call someone to come and get them. In the meantime, near the city limits, one of our fellow officers apprehended the real convenience store robbers.

We had a rather irate woman call 911 because she wanted the neighbors upstairs from her arrested for flushing the toilet too loudly.

A local merchant came to the station to report a wedding invitation he found outside in his dumpster that wasn't his. He wanted us to arrest the people for putting trash in his garbage dumpster.

The young male who identified himself as the boyfriend of a local married woman called us because he wanted her husband arrested for coming home early from work without calling first or announcing himself. The husband had interrupted the wife and her lover on several different occasions and the young man had to hide in the closet to avoid being detected. He was claustrophobic, and being stuck in the confined area for any period of time was extremely stressful for the man.

My horse is my best friend out here on the city streets, but sometimes your friends don't always behave themselves. One very hot summer day, I tied her up outside a neighborhood market to go inside and get a bottle of water. No sooner had I gotten inside when this woman comes in and yells to me that my horse is stealing some woman's purse. I quickly ran outside to see my horse with the lady's straw purse in its mouth and the woman holding the strap, trying to get it back. It was rather humorous. Fortunately the woman's purse wasn't damaged and she was a good sport about it. I guess it looked like dinner to my horse.

I've found that using a video camera while sitting near stop signs can be very useful in court. There is no question if a stop was made or not. While in court for a stop sign violation one day, I played the tape of the defendant going through the stop sign three times for the judge. When the defense attorney asked to play the video tape again, the judge said, "She didn't stop the first three times, you think she's going to stop this time? Guilty!"

Early one evening I stopped a young woman for speeding in a residential zone. She asked me to please hurry and just give her a ticket because she knew she was speeding. I asked her why she was in such a hurry and she said, "I had to get milk for my baby. She's only three months old and I don't want to leave her alone that long." She'd just run to the store to buy some milk which I could see on the front seat. I inquired if anyone was at home with the baby and she said, "No." We were a few blocks away from her house, so I told her to just drive home and feed the baby; I'd finish the ticket when I get there. She zoomed off and I followed. When I got to the door a few minutes later, she quickly opened the door and asked me in to see her baby. There on the floor was the cutest baby kitten I'd ever seen. Apparently the woman was single and she referred to her small feline as "Baby."

I stopped a suspicious vehicle and found that the two occupants were in possession of drugs and drug paraphernalia. When I asked the driver for his name and date of birth as he was handing me his license, he gave me a different name than the one on the license. It was his picture on the document, though. I asked again, and he insisted it was a different one than the name I read to him off the license. Sometimes people are so ridiculous. We just added another charge to his arrest. Don't they think we can read, or check on the information they give to us?

Early one afternoon, I was radioed about a local resident's alarm being tripped. As soon as I heard the address, I knew exactly which house it was. I was acquainted with the owners only informally, but was quite familiar with the beautiful historical house and its extraordinary doorbell chimes. When I pulled up to the house, I quickly exited my cruiser and proceeded with caution to inspect the exterior of the dwelling. I saw no visible signs of forced entry or any suspicious vehicles in the immediate vicinity. I then proceeded to walk up to the front door and ring the chimes and let the resident know—if they were home—that everything appeared fine. No one came to the door. I then went around back to knock on the kitchen door. As I rounded the corner, I walked smack into a man with a pillowcase full of, as we later determined, the occupant's stolen possessions. He fell flat on his back and I instinctively pulled my sidearm. The second suspect was exiting the house and immediately dropped the stereo he was carrying and raised his gloved hands. My back-up arrived shortly afterwards. Apparently, the doorbell chimes spooked the robbers and they decided to exit the dwelling—quickly. They also had previously stolen the neighbor's spare keys that were hidden under the door mat. There was no need for a getaway vehicle, because they lived next door in the second floor apartment.

A man checked into a local motel for the night. The next morning he went to the front desk clerk and robbed him at gun point. He then proceeded to return to his room. When we arrived we found him sitting on the end of the bed, watching television. He admitted to robbing the employee because he needed more money to pay for an extra night. It seems that he liked the room and the numerous cable channels he could watch.

Around two in the morning I saw this vehicle being driven by a young woman who was unable to keep her lane. She would drive across the center line and then cross over almost into the gutter. I quickly pulled her over and then another car following her stopped ahead of her vehicle on the side of the road. The female from the first car got out, came running over to me and indicated she had everything under control. I asked her what she was referring to and she said that her friend was the one I had originally pulled over. Motioning to the other vehicle, the young woman said, "My friend is really drunk and I didn't want her to drive home alone. So I'm following her to make sure she isn't in an accident." The woman was under the belief that the slogan, "Friends don't let friends drive drunk" didn't mean that the person couldn't drive a car while drunk. It meant as long as someone they knew was following them, then they weren't alone. I didn't know which one was the worst to have driving on the road—the drunk or the completely clueless "friend."

One night, I saw a van parked in a secluded spot. I got out of my cruiser and knocked on the window. I could detect commotion in the back, but no one was visible from where I stood. I knocked again. Finally, I opened the unlocked driver side door, identified myself as a police officer and asked the occupants to please get dressed and step outside the vehicle. The two people, a rather rotund female in her thirties and an eighteen year old male, who couldn't weigh more than 120 pounds, stepped out. The young man kept thanking me for showing up and rescuing him. Evidently, the obese woman was having sex with him while she had him pinned to the floor with his head wedged under the seat for almost an hour. He was unable to move. The poor kid even had an indentation across his forehead from the bar under the seat.

Late one night we pulled this very drunk middle-aged woman over for DUI. She had been swerving so much that her entire car would go into the other lane and then swerve back into her own lane. When we asked her to get out of the car, she squinted at us. She obliged but asked if she could get something out of the back seat. We inquired as to what was it that she really needed to have. She said, while slurring, that she needed to put in her eye back in. The woman had tossed her glass eye into the back seat of the car before she left the bar. No wonder why she was squinting so much.

On one occasion, my partner and I were dispatched to a home on the complaint of a large crowd gathered out front of the residence. The address given was in a quiet residential neighborhood. The complainant was an elderly gentleman who lived alone. Upon arriving to the scene, we observed nothing out of the ordinary. We knocked on the front door and were met by the complainant. He then looked around the front yard and whispered into my ear, "Did you see them?" Realizing the old man was somewhat disoriented, we placated him by telling him that we chased them all away. The old man then told us that they were inside his house. We then entered his house and feigned the idea of shooing away a large crowd of people. As we were about to leave the old man thanked us, however, he again whispered to my partner that there was still one man sleeping in his bed. We then went into his bedroom and used our nightsticks, flailing at the mattress and yelling, "Get out of this man's house!" My partner then did his world-famous Jackie Gleason impression before we left. As we were leaving out the front door, the old man whispered into my partner's ear, "You know I love your show, The Honeymooners. Are you still married to Alice?"

One afternoon a number of years ago, I was patrolling the area in and around the local park, when a short Asian woman who appeared very distraught came over to my cruiser. Apparently it was her birthday and she and her boyfriend (who was of Jewish heritage) were eloping. Unfortunately the justice of the peace they'd hired didn't show up. I asked if they had their marriage license and they did. Being a bit of a romantic, I made a few phone calls and through the help of fellow officers, was able to track down another Justice of the Peace. The sun was setting by the time the 70 year-old man arrived, wearing a tux. I used the spotlight from my cruiser as illumination and I was also asked to be the best man. Just as the ceremony was about to begin, the groundskeeper at the park came over and told us that we'd have to leave the park unless we had a permit or he'd call the police. I motioned to my cruiser and told him that the police were already here and the situation was under control. The couple was married and the husband and I have been friends ever since.

The owner of a local tavern called the police department because he was concerned about an item one of his regular customers had brought into the bar that evening: a mortar shell with barnacles on it that he'd found washed up on the town beach. When we arrived, the bar patron and several of his friends were in the corner scraping off the barnacles using a chisel and hammer that one of them had fetched from the tool chest on the back of their pick-up truck. We called the bomb squad in to retrieve the mortar shell which was about one-foot in length. Later it was determined that the shell was indeed still live and could have exploded at any time.

The woman indicated that she was fine, just a little embarrassed, when we arrived at the scene of the one-car accident. She had driven her late model vehicle through several construction barriers and into the sink hole which had appeared during the night. The woman said she didn't pay attention as much as she should have while driving, because her bra hook had somehow come undone and she was trying to fix it while driving in morning rush hour traffic. By the time she saw the barriers, it was too late. Crunch.

We were dispatched to a local residence because the owner was believed to have died at home of natural causes. Upon entering the dwelling, we not only found the body of the woman, but thousands of empty beer cans stacked in every room of the house. We could barely get to the woman's body because the empty cans were lined up three to four feet high and deep. In one back bedroom, once the beer cans were removed, you could tell that no one had entered that room for years; everything was neatly in its place.

———

I dislike being dispatched to suicides, but the worst scenes are the ones where the person had failed in their first attempt and succeeded in their subsequent attempt. For instance, a young man in his early thirties was distraught over the break-up with his girlfriend and decided to kill himself. His method of death was to use a table saw. Apparently, he placed his head on the table saw bench facing the blade and turned on the saw. It had gotten stuck part way through his face, so he had to pull his head out and do it again. This time he succeeded. There was blood and tissue everywhere. I can't imagine how anyone could kill themselves, let alone in this manner.

———

Domestic fights break out for the most ridiculous reasons. One Thanksgiving were dispatched to a residence in a normally quiet neighborhood, because the wife had attempted to cook the turkey without defrosting it first. This was her first Thanksgiving with the relatives visiting for the holiday, and she'd never cooked a turkey before. There had been name-calling by the father-in-law in reference to the lack of intelligence by his daughter-in-law. The husband took offense at his father's words and decked the father. The father then tried to hit his son, but missed and struck his own wife—the son's stepmother. Screaming ensued as food was thrown, dishes smashed and bones were broken. When we arrived, two ambulances were needed to transport the relatives to the hospital for everything from several broken noses to an uncle suffering from a heart attack. All this because the woman was inexperienced at cooking a turkey.

One rainy summer evening we were summoned to an upscale restaurant because one of the guests was causing a disturbance. The attractive young woman had removed her raincoat at a table near the front window and, unknown to her other companions, was wearing only her "birthday suit" underneath. They attempted to get her to put her wrap back on, but she refused. When my partner and I arrived, we were met in the front lobby by the woman wrapped in a white table cloth, and her friends trying to get her out the door. One of her companions was exchanging information with the owner to cover the damages she'd caused during their attempt to remove her from the restaurant. Once we walked her out the door and towards the cruiser, she wrestled herself free from our grip—and the tablecloth. The woman then fell to the wet pavement and rolled underneath the police car—naked. By this time, it's pouring rain, she refuses to come out from underneath the car, and a crowd is gathering around the front of the restaurant. My supervisor arrived at the scene and tried to coax her out from under the vehicle. After about 20 minutes we were able to get her out and into the ambulance. She was then taken to the hospital for psychiatric observation and also to have her bruises and scrapes attended to.

This one citizen in town always thought she was dirty, even though she was clean. She was seen constantly cleaning and scrubbing her hands. She scrubbed her hands so frequently that sometimes they would bleed from the constant rubbing. When we were dispatched to her apartment for a routine call, we found that she had been cleaning her hands with a tissue and rubbing alcohol. After she used the tissue, she threw it into a particular room. The pile of tissues in there was literally four-feet high. Not only was it a health hazard, but a fire hazard as well. We had to call in professionals from the State that deal with hazardous materials to remove the tissues from her dwelling. It's a good thing she didn't smoke.

A man broke into a bank after hours and instead of stealing currency, stole the bank's video camera instead. Unknown to the thief at the time, the camera was videotaping him as he removed it from its position. The recorder was located elsewhere in the bank, so he didn't get the videotape of himself stealing the camera, but the bank officials did.

A man walked into a local convenience store, put a $20 bill on the counter and asked for change. When the clerk opened the cash drawer, the man pulled a gun and demanded all the money in the register. The clerk quickly handed over the cash. The man fled, leaving his original $20 bill on the counter. The total amount he got from the cashier was only $15; he lost $5 committing the crime.

A thief wearing a ski mask and carrying a gun burst into the bank during business hours. He pointed his gun at the security guard and yelled, "FREEZE, MOTHER-STICKERS, THIS IS A F**K-UP!" At first everyone was quiet. Then the snickers started. The security guard doubled over laughing at the robber's mixed up words. The thief turned and ran out the door. He was not apprehended and is still at large. In memory of the event, the bank later put a plaque on the wall engraved "Freeze, Mother-stickers, this is a f**k-up!"

A man attempted to steal gasoline by siphoning it from a motorhome which was parked on a local street. When the police arrived at the scene, they found the man in agony, curled up next to a motorhome near spilled sewage. The man admitted to trying to steal gasoline but had plugged his hose into the motorhome's sewage tank by mistake.

A guy who just had to have some beer decided to rob the local liquor store. He decided that the easiest way to enter would be to thrown a cinder block through the front window, grab the liquor and run. What the would-be robber did not know was that the front window was made of Plexiglass. When he toss the cinder block at it, the cinder block bounced back and hit the man in the head, knocking him unconscious. The entire incident was captured on the store's surveillance cameras.

As a female customer left a local convenience store, a man snatched her purse and fled. The clerk called 911 immediately and the woman was able to give a detailed description of the thief. Within minutes, the crook was apprehended and driven back to the store. The thief was then taken out of the cruiser and told to stand there for a positive ID. Seeing the woman, the thief admitted freely, "Yes Officer . . . that's her. That's the lady I stole the purse from."

A woman who had reported her car stolen mentioned that her car phone was also in it. The officer taking the report called the car phone number and posed as someone who had read an ad about the car being for sale and was interested in purchasing it. They made arrangements to meet, and the thief was promptly arrested.

A would-be thief walked into a fast food restaurant during breakfast hours and flashed a gun at the cashier demanding cash. The clerk said they could not open the cash register without a food order. The armed man complied and ordered onion rings. The cashier then responded that they did not serve onion rings for breakfast. The man got frustrated, and left the restaurant without money . . . or onion rings.

Routine Calls?

ACCIDENTS & INCIDENTS

"What was the most bizarre accident or incident you ever witnessed or were called to?" is the topic of this chapter. This is one of those questions that a number of officers decided to pass on. It is understandable when they've seen so many people injured or dying, or worse yet, dead and in a number of pieces. The memories and flashbacks they have concerning a number of accidents is all too common for those in law enforcement.

I've written this chapter without much graphic detail. I'm sure you can use your imagination as to what a scene would probably look like where someone has been killed. If you want blood and guts, it would be best if you rented a movie. The officers did describe to me in detail a number of accidents and a few even showed me pictures of the remains of what used to be cars and trucks. For a few officers, it was overwhelming to recount particular accidents, especially the ones where they were unable to save the lives of those injured or trapped within burning vehicles.

The officer has to maintain control of a situation without letting his or her personal feelings or emotions get in the way. At the scene of an accident, it is the job of the officer to get the facts, while providing comfort to those injured until the ambulance arrives. One thing in particular that adds more aggravation to an already distressing situation are those people passing the accident who find it necessary to rubberneck. People want to see the blood, guts and gore. When the passerby slows down and impedes traffic while an officer is trying to save the lives of those injured, it just makes the situation worse. Whenever you see an accident where the officers have already arrived at the scene, don't stop to take a look. You'll end up causing a traffic back-up and potentially even be the cause of additional accidents. Be responsible; let those officers and medical personnel do their jobs. Imagine if it were you or a loved one that was injured in an accident. Wouldn't you want the officers to be paying attention to your needs, instead of having to go over to the stopped motorist and tell them to keep moving? Too often, accidents are life and death situations.

Also, please remember that driving a car is a privilege which carries an enormous amount of responsibility. Your life and the lives of your passengers, as well as other motorists, are the responsibility of the driver. Pay attention. Obey the laws. Slow down for construction workers. But most important of all, don't drink and drive.

In a one-car accident, a man ran over a road sign and sideswiped a tree. Apparently he'd taken a sip of his soda from the newly-opened can and some of the bubbles went up his nose. He then dropped the can in his lap, and it spilled as he sneezed. It was then that he lifted his posterior off the seat and accidentally depressed the accelerator to the floor, ran over a sign and sideswiped a big oak tree. He sustained only minor injuries, since he was wearing his seat belt at the time, but totaled his car.

We arrived at the scene of a construction accident to find a man lying on the ground, screaming in pain. The ambulance was en route. Apparently he and several other workers were coming down off the roof they'd been shingling using electric nail guns. They usually waited until the other person was completely off the ladder before descending it themselves. But today was Friday, the night they went to the local tavern before they each went home, and they were all in a rush. One of the workers was carrying his nail gun without the safety lock on, as he climbed down the ladder. He got his leg caught on a dangling wire and squeezed the trigger as he fell four feet or so to the ground. The nail gun then shot the accident victim with a nail, right in the crotch. It hurts just thinking about it. The first man was O. K., though.

A young toddler was playing on the couch near the drapes; somehow he'd gotten the cord wrapped around his neck and then slipped off the couch. The mother found the child, blue and not breathing. She had only left the room to get her checkbook from upstairs. He's alive right now, but in intensive care at the children's hospital. Baby-proof your house!

A man's car had a dead battery and he tried jump-starting it while it was in the two-car garage attached to the house. Well, he apparently crossed the wires and a small fire started in the engine. He pushed the flaming auto out of the garage and into the street. A neighbor called 911 and we responded to the car fire, and subsequent house fire—a spark had flown onto a mattress leaning against the garage wall, and had caught fire. The blaze then spread to the main house, and the garden hose the man was using to extinguish the fire wasn't even making a dent. The fire department arrived and extinguished the car, garage and house fires. The fire marshal then began inspecting the two-story turn-of-the-century house room by room to make sure there was no longer any danger of fire. He came upon a locked oak door on the second floor near the back staircase, which the man refused to unlock. He said he didn't have the key; his roommate did. We informed him that if he didn't comply, we'd have to break it down. He then removed the key from a chain around his neck and unlocked the door. When we opened it, we were literally "blinded by the light." Inside the room were four high-intensity lamps (the type found in auditoriums) hanging from the high ceiling. The marijuana plants were several feet high. The man and his roommate were growing the illegal substance inside the spare bedroom. All this from a dead battery.

A young teenage girl and her friend decided to steal a car. We saw her speed past us and we pursued. She slowed the car down and decided to bail out. But she tripped, and fell into the path of the car and got her arm run over by the same vehicle she'd just stolen. What irony!

My embarrassing moment was when I had to go home and change into another set of pants because I'd ripped them right up the back while arresting a drunk. On my way home I saw a woman speeding, not wearing her seat belt and two children in the car not in their car seats. I pulled her over, and went to the car window in order to lecture her. While leaning on the frame, another car drove by and honked their horn. It's then that I remembered that my valentine boxer's were "blowing in the wind." Backing up towards my car I called to the woman, "Speeding, no seat belt and kids not in car seats." Without saying another word, I got back into the car and drove off. I forgot to tell the woman she could leave.

A pit bull had attacked a small child and inflicted multiple cuts and lacerations over her face and body which would require hundreds of stitches and plastic surgery to repair. We were summoned to find the pit bull that had taken off into the neighborhood—and put it down. When we finally caught up with the vicious animal, it attacked us. These dogs are so strong and ruthless, it took seven bullets and 20 minutes before the dog passed away.

While patrolling the snowy city streets one very cold February morning, I saw a naked man walking down the sidewalk and approaching several pedestrians. They just kept walking. I pulled up next to them and asked what the male "Godiva" had asked. They indicated he was looking for drugs. I thanked them and proceed to call in my naked guy. I got out and asked him to get into my cruiser. I retrieved a blanket from the trunk and had him wrap himself up. On my way to the station, he started making noises. I couldn't see what he was doing and when I finally realized it, it was too late. He had not only defecated on the blanket, but also gave himself a "hand job." Sometimes people are disgusting.

A local teenage kid in the neighborhood locked himself out of his house one Friday night when his parents were out to dinner. He decided to climb down the chimney because he didn't want to damage a window. Obviously he didn't get far. He got stuck a few feet down and ended up being trapped for several hours before his parents came home and called us and the fire department.

A man driving a Camaro had slammed his car sideways into a telephone pole and the car split in half upon impact. When we arrived at the scene, the driver of the totaled vehicle was sound asleep in the front half of the car. He was oblivious as to what had happened, and was completely uninjured.

We arrested and brought in a woman in wearing a housecoat for attempted assault, resisting arrest, and a number of other related charges. Before she was put in the cell, a female police officer had to search her for hidden "items." No sooner had we walked out the door than we heard the female officer scream. Rushing back in, she informed us that during the course of the body search, she'd discovered that the person was really a man in drag.

We had received a call that a man had died of natural causes while at home. As I rang the doorbell, sitting on the porch in a rocking chair was a gentleman, relaxing. I said, "Good morning, sir," then proceeded to make small talk until a woman came and opened the front door. I went inside to get all the pertinent information from the wife of the deceased. I introduced myself and extended my condolences for her loss. I then asked, "Where is your husband now, ma'am?" She immediately got this quizzical look on her face and said, "He's on the porch in the rocking chair, of course." It then dawned on me that the polite gentleman on the front porch hadn't spoken a word.

I arrived at the scene of a two-car accident. The driver in the first car suffered only minor injuries. The second car's passenger wasn't as fortunate. The front passenger was thrown into the back seat of the car, and the driver was pinned by the engine with her hands still holding the steering wheel. The car looked like an accordion. I told the female driver that an ambulance was on the way, as well as fire rescue to help get her unpinned. She looked right at me, tried to start the demolished vehicle and said, "We were just leaving, officer." The woman was in shock.

We had received a call of someone breaking and entering a home, with the teenage son reporting the call from the house while the intruders were still inside. The young man had barricaded himself in the bathroom, without being seen by them, and had called 911. Four cruisers rushed to the scene as the boy stayed on the line with the dispatch. We couldn't find any sign of forced entry and asked the boy to come unlock the front door and let us in. He was terrified and refused to leave the safety of the second-floor bathroom. He insisted he could still hear them in one of the rooms. We then asked him to come to the window. I was the lucky one who had to shimmy up to the second-floor window because he was too afraid to come down, ripping my pants in the meantime. When I joined the young man, I too could hear rummaging in the other room. I radioed the other officers that I was going to open the front door to let them in. As I came out of the bathroom and rounded the corner, I came face to face (in a manner of speaking) with the perpetrator—a squirrel! He stood up on two feet and screamed. I screamed louder. Boy was I glad my shift was over.

I was out training one of the rookies on the force on how to properly stop a citizen and write a speeding ticket in an efficient manner. He stopped the woman, got the pertinent documents and headed back to the cruiser. He quickly wrote the ticket and before bringing it back to the motorist, asked me to take a quick look at it. I told him everything was fine, except for the fact that he'd written the ticket out to himself. I guess I made the poor guy a little nervous.

Another officer radioed in that he'd found an 8-foot pipe bomb while walking his beat. Our antiquated dispatch radio had more static than normal, so we had him repeat his first transmission. Immediately we called in the bomb squad and cleared the neighborhood of all non-police personnel. Once the bomb squad got there the officer asked curiously why they were there. One replied, "Because of the 8-foot pipe bomb." The officer then told them, "No, I said I found an 8-foot *python*." The town funds for our new radio system were finally available the next fiscal year.

In the middle of winter in the northeast, a nude man was walking down the street, acting like nothing was wrong. When we arrived, he took off and we followed. He then proceeded to jump into the half-frozen river and swam across. We never caught up to him.

Around seven in the morning, this young female medical student was jogging down the city sidewalk wearing her Walkman, when she saw a car drive up onto the sidewalk directly towards her. She apparently tried to run out of the path of the oncoming vehicle, but was hit and thrown up onto the hood of the car and then onto the windshield. The driver of the vehicle then proceeded to smash into another parked car. When we arrived at the accident scene, the driver told us that the jogger was responsible for her hitting the other parked car. If the pedestrian wasn't blocking her vision she might have been able to avoid hitting the parked car. It didn't seem to faze her that she'd just driven down a sidewalk and slammed into a person. The victim later indicated that she scrunched up into the fetal position and protected her head with her hands as she was hit. She had no serious injuries other than to her kneecaps, and strained and pulled muscles.

We stopped a very intoxicated individual very shortly after he'd left the bar. He'd driven his vehicle into the light post across the street. He argued that he wasn't "drinking and driving." He'd drunk all the alcohol at the bar and he would never drink and drive since he drives a standard-shift and would be unable to hold a glass while shifting.

One night, we were patrolling a warehouse in an industrial area and noticed that a side door was left wide open. We got out to investigate. We went inside and looked around. Seeing and hearing nothing suspicious on the first floor, we got in the freight elevator and took it to the top floor to continue our investigation from the top down. The one thing we were not aware of was that when the warehouse is closed, the freight elevator will go up, but the doors won't open and it will not go down. It was a safety measure taken by the company to insure that if their place was broken into, no one would be able to get out the elevator. My partner and I can safely state that it is highly effective. We had to radio for help to come and get us out of the elevator. Incidentally, no one was found in the building and nothing was ever reported missing.

We arrived at the scene of a house fire. No one was hurt, but the young woman was understandably shaken up. She said she had been in the kitchen baking brownies. The phone rang and she went into the den to answer it. When she got off the phone she noticed that smoke was pouring out of the kitchen and that the microwave plug and part of the wall was on fire. She had placed the brownies in the microwaves to bake for 30 minutes. She'd been following the recipe for baking in the oven, not the microwave, and that's how the fire got started.

When I arrived at the scene of the one-car accident, I found the driver to be an 80 year-old man who was more interested in finding his pipe that he'd lost during his abrupt stop with a telephone pole and parked car, than the condition of his grandson, his car or himself. The young boy, strapped in the front passenger seat said that hitting the pole and car was his fault. I asked him why he felt it was his fault. He said "Whenever I ride with grandpa, I'm supposed to pay attention as to when grandpa plans on lighting his pipe. He takes both hands off the wheel without saying a word and lets me steer while he lights his pipe and keeps his foot on the gas. I've done it for the past few years—since I was six years old. Today I was looking out the window at kids playing baseball, when I should have been watching grandpa. I'm sorry." I'm just glad the boy was all right.

I was in court and told the judge that the defendant for my red light violation case had dropped the judge's name as being a very close friend of his. Not that it would have made a difference when I stopped him. It turned out that the judge didn't know him, and he really didn't know the judge, either. He was pronounced guilty.

A robber shot himself with his own gun while trying to rob a local car wash. He'd gotten into a struggle with the attendant, the trigger got pulled, and the thief was shot. He died several days later.

A bouncer at a nearby café witnessed a criminal attempt a carjacking and the and attacking the driver—with a gun ready to shoot him. The bouncer thought fast and shot the criminal. The shooting was justified and the criminal was apprehended and hospitalized.

I went to a picnic that was hosted by friends of my wife. A guy introduced himself to me and said somebody told him I was a police officer. He asked all kinds of questions: what department, what area I patrolled and so on. He hit me as a nobody who thinks he's somebody.

They were building a new four-lane divided highway through my area. It was all done, but not open to the public yet. People were using it as a short cut and we were citing people for driving on the closed highway. Well, now I stop this guy that I'd met only once at the picnic. He asked what department I was from. When I told him, he said, "Do you know Officer XYZ? He works for your department. I know him. We do a lot of stuff together; go to picnics and stuff." I said, "Yeah, I know Officer XYZ," and proceeded to write him a ticket for driving on the closed highway, signing my name very neatly and clearly. I handed him the ticket and sent him on his way fast. I have often wondered what his reaction was when he saw my name, "Officer XYZ," as the issuing officer.

A local driver's education instructor ordered a female driving student of his to pursue a car that had cut them off. The instructor then assaulted the other driver once they'd caught up to him. The student driver wasn't ticketed, but the instructor was ticketed, arrested, then released on bond. He said he was just angry that the other driver had cut them off.

A cab driver was found lying next to his cab, bleeding and bruised from apparent stab wounds. He stated that three passengers mugged him and left him lying in the roadway. But under further questioning, he confessed that he'd lost all his employer's money while gambling and had caused all the injuries to himself. He was charged with filing a false police report.

We had a case of an accidental drowning of an elderly woman and her dog. It seems that the woman was mowing her back yard and exercising her dog, which she'd tied to the mower. The woman accidentally got entangled in her dog's chain and fell into the small backyard pond she was cutting grass near. They both died.

Three female high school students were shocked when one day while staying after school to do research in the library, they came across the custodian, wandering naked through the school.

An overzealous fan decided to hang his favorite baseball team's banner from a commuter train overpass, wishing them luck. He was hit by the train while attempting to hang it. His friend escaped injury, but he died.

A man who slept with his .38 revolver next to him on his night stand was awakened by the phone ringing. He reached over to pick up the receiver and accidentally grabbed the weapon, which discharged as he brought it to his ear. He died instantly.

A stressed out mail carrier assaulted and seriously injured a jogger who made degrading remarks concerning his occupation. The mail carrier pick up a rake left on a nearby resident's lawn and started hitting the jogger on the head. The assailant turned himself in and claimed that he was under a lot of stress as a result of his job.

A motorist was caught in an automated speed trap that measures speed using radar and photographs the car. A ticket was then sent to his address. Instead of payment, he sent the police department a photocopy of a $40.00 bill. Several days later, he received a letter from the police department that contained another picture, one of handcuffs. He paid the fine.

An angry man was using a shotgun like a club to break a former girlfriend's windshield. He shot himself when the gun discharged accidently. It killed him instantly.

Two wannabe mechanics decided to drive their farm truck down a local highway while one of them hung underneath so they could find out what was making all the racket. The daredevil's clothes became entangled and the driver found him "wrapped around the drive shaft." Dead.

A cigarette lighter was the cause of the man's untimely death. He was having firing problems with a rather large caliber gun and used his lighter to check inside the barrel of the .54- caliber muzzle loader. The gun powder exploded and the weapon discharged in his face. The explosion killed him.

A man was being disorderly inside a local food market. When the cashier threatened to call us, the thief grabbed a hot dog, shoved it into his mouth whole and walked out the door without paying for it. He was found unconscious in front of the store. The paramedics removed the six-inch wiener from the man's throat but it was too late. He'd choked to death.

Two people were vandalizing an electric tower by disassembling it with wrenches. The teens were apparently planning to sell the stolen aluminum at a local scrap yard. One of the thieves was crushed to death as the tower came crashing down on them. The second one survived being buried under the five-ton tower by digging himself out.

One evening a woman's son and his friend asked to have the car moved so they could play basketball in the driveway; the car was in the way. The mother allowed her juvenile son to back the family car down the driveway as she directed the youngster from behind the moving vehicle. She accidentally lost her balance and fell backwards into the bushes. Her son lost sight of her and hit the gas pedal instead of the brake, running her over. She died as a result of her injuries.

A man in his early twenties died as a result of a bungee cord accident. He decided to bungee jump off a railroad trestle by taping a bunch of bungee cords together and strapping the end around one foot and the other to the train trestle. The cord he'd assembled was greater than the distance from the bridge to the ground. He ended up killing himself.

Instead of calling someone to help him retrieve his car keys, a man was found dead from drowning after sticking his head through an 18-inch wide sewer grate. There was only two feet of water.

A safety-conscious man decided to tie a rope around himself and attach it to the bumper of his car while he climbed on the roof to fix his antenna. He didn't tell his wife what he'd done and she got in the car to go to the store. The man was yanked off the roof and dragged quite a distance before a passerby stopped the wife to let her know that she was dragging her husband. He survived after spending several weeks in the hospital.

A distraught woman went out and bought a chain saw, knife, rifle, bullets and a video on how to use the weapons. On the fateful day, she stopped and bought a pizza on her way home. She then proceeded to kill her husband while he was napping in bed, came downstairs and fed the kids their pizza. Later, she crawled into bed with her dead husband and tried (unsuccessfully) to kill herself. The woman was upset about her husband's extramarital affairs.

After they smashed up their vehicle, the uninjured driver and a back-seat passenger called for a tow truck. Their other friend had been drinking heavily and was sleeping it off so they rode in the cab with the tow truck driver while they left their friend in the car being towed to the owner's residence. It's there they discovered that their female friend was in fact dead. It was later determined that she died instantly as a result of a broken neck she had sustained from the earlier crash.

A young male child lost his grip and fell to his death off a 100-foot cliff after swinging on a cross that marked the spot where another person had died. It's sad.

A thief with a rather extensive arrest record died when he fell face first through the ceiling of a bicycle shop he was burglarizing. He'd decided to carry his flashlight in his mouth while attempting to gain entry to the shop, and when he fell and subsequently landed on the floor, his illuminator was pushed to the back of his skull.

An avid jogger died after accidentally running off a 200-foot cliff on his daily route. His wife indicated that he was often preoccupied with other thoughts while running and didn't always pay that much attention to what was going on around him. Apparently not.

A young female with a passion for animals accidentally hit a deer with her car. The vehicle was completely demolished; fortunately she was unharmed. I indicated to her that for humane reasons, I had to shoot the deer because it had two broken legs and possibly internal bleeding. She immediately ran to the deer's rescue, grabbed it around the neck and hugged the animal. That's when the deer bucked her and broke her nose. The deer was about 150 pounds and still strong enough even though it was dying. The girl didn't want me to kill the deer and kept blocking my aim. I didn't know whether to shoot the deer or her.

A guy accidentally shot his friend with a .22-caliber gun while trying to kill an insect. The guy aimed his gun, shot, and the bullet ricocheted off a rock near the creature and hit his friend in the skull. The victim sustained a fractured skull, but survived.

While out on patrol one night, I spotted in the distance a bright light surrounding an object hovering in the sky. As I drove closer to it, another officer pulled up next to me. We both got out and speculated as to what we were seeing. We both agreed that it definitely wasn't from this world, especially since it shot away as silently and quickly as it had arrived.

A teenage juvenile shot his sister with a .22-caliber pistol because he wanted to use the phone and was upset that she was monopolizing it. Fortunately, the sister suffered only minor injuries.

_____

When I first came around the corner, I could see the vehicle wasn't in that bad a shape, but enough to need a tow. It was wedged between a large rock and a tall tree, with a flat tire and a very intoxicated man behind the wheel. Fortunately, he was wearing his seat belt, and had no visible signs of injury. As I leaned in closer to make sure he was all right while we waited for the ambulance, the odor of alcohol almost knocked me out. He reeked. I inquired as to why he drove and didn't call a cab or a friend to drive him home. He said a "friend" was driving. I asked, "If you weren't driving, then who was?" He insisted it was his dog which was lying calmly next on the passenger seat next to him.

_____

A wealthy resident came by the station to let us know that she was going out of town for a few months and would appreciate it if we would look after her historic house to make sure that no one burglarized it while she was away. She was kind enough to give us her itinerary, just in case there was a problem. Every few days, we'd take a look around her property and check for any signs of forced entry. We live in a rather rural area, and crime is almost nonexistent. Less than a week after she'd left, we had the unfortunate task of calling and notifying her that someone did in fact do damage to her property. Several windows had been smashed, but it didn't appear that anything was taken. The odd part was that the windows were broken from the inside; the glass was scattered about on the grass below the windows. We put plywood over the broken windows and nailed them down. She'd asked that we padlock her doors and if possible, nail down all the windows on the first floor; she would reimburse us when she returned. I had the only key. I returned the following day to inspect the premises and I spied that several more windows were smashed. They too, like the first, had been broken from the inside out. I called for back-up and we both inspected the house. No one had entered—since I had the key—all the doors were padlocked, and the windows nailed shut. Upon investigating, no living person was found to be within the house.

While investigating a burglary we found part of the person who'd attempted to steal the safe—their finger. The half-ton safe they were trying to steal slipped and caught his finger, severing it. The owner of the digit was easily found by calling local hospitals. The finger was brought to the hospital where the thief was being treated but it was too late for it to be reattached. He literally left his finger prints at the scene of the crime.

At a family reunion, two cousins began wrestling with each other. It started off friendly, but later turned into an assault. One of the cousins actually bit off a piece of his relative's tongue. It wasn't able to be surgically reattached. And the biter was arrested and charged with assault.

A man was seen entering the house of a neighbor by breaking a window, near the back door. The watchful neighbor called to report the situation. When we arrived, the man was exiting the house with a small sack of stolen articles. We then went on a foot chase, through back yards and over hedges. The final stretch of the pursuit was climbing a 10-foot high wire fence that had rust and several broken metal pieces projecting upwards. The guy made it over the fence before we could catch him, but fortunately my partner had anticipated his route and captured him on the other side. We read him his rights and brought him to the station. As he stood next to me, a puddle of blood was accumulating on the floor near his feet. It was finally determined—after we brought him to the emergency room—that when he'd tried to scale the fence his testicles had gotten caught and ripped off. We went back to the scene and sure enough, there they were, dangling on the top jagged pieces of metal. By the time we were able to retrieve them and get them to the hospital, it was too late for the doctors to reattach them. The man had been on drugs and was totally clueless about the mutilation he'd done to his body.

A man robbed a bank which is located next to a fast food restaurant. The crook who stole the money was apprehended a short time later in the restaurant next door eating his cheeseburger.

An elderly gentleman driving with his wife felt threatened by the occupants of another car. He reached for the gun he kept under the front seat, hoping to scare them away, but accidentally shot his wife instead.

While driving on the freeway, a woman in the center lane put on her left signal and immediately slammed into my cruiser. When we came to a stop, she started yelling at me and said that the accident was my fault. She was under the impression that once she put her turn signal on, she had the right of way and everybody is supposed to move out of her way. I didn't move, and since she wanted to be in my lane, she hit my vehicle. She honestly believed it was her right to hit my cruiser.

The decapitated head of a homeless man was found near a dumpster, but the rest of his body wasn't recovered from the local landfill until several days later. The man was apparently sleeping in the dumpster on the day the garbage man emptied the large metal container into his truck. The worker was unaware of the slumbering man because the operator picks up the garbage bin and dumps the rubbish by pushing buttons from inside the vehicle.

Two men decided to steal an ATM machine outside a local bank by wrapping chains around the machine and towing it away with their pick-up truck. They were unsuccessful at their attempt. The only thing that moved when they hit the accelerator was the bumper off the back of their pick-up. They drove away leaving their chain, bumper and license plate which was secured to the bumper.

It's amazing how such a small creature like a squirrel can be the cause of thousands of dollars worth of needed automotive repairs. Recently a young woman driving a late model Mercedes slammed on her brakes on a major highway to avoid hitting the little creature and as a result created a three-car pile-up. The squirrel escaped without injury; unfortunately the same could not be said about the people driving and riding in the crunched vehicles.

It almost never fails that when there is an accident on a divided highway or thoroughfare in our county, some idiot on the other side is going to rubberneck in hopes of seeing some injured individual lying on the side of the road or still trapped in the smashed automobile. A man who was rubbernecking and going the opposite direction took his eyes off the road and slammed into a utility pole on the other side of the highway. The emergency crew had to stop traffic now in both directions to attend to the new accident. He totaled his car and had some serious facial injuries from hitting the windshield and not wearing a seat belt. As he was being placed in the ambulance he complained about the other motorists watching him being transported into the emergency vehicle. How ironic. I bet he stopped rubbernecking, at least until his injuries were healed.

We came upon a one-car accident where the driver had driven down an embankment and into the a small wading pond located in the local park. The woman had a difficult time getting out of the standard shift vehicle because she was in a leg cast from her foot to her thigh. She had attempted to drive the car on her own—even though it was impossible to shift the vehicle—because she was tired of imposing on other people's kindness in chauffeuring her around while her leg healed.

Being with the mounted police here in the city has an enormous amount of benefits, including being able to talk with the local adults and even children. Sometimes, though my horse gets a little antsy about people touching her mouth without petting her first. I told this particular woman that it probably wouldn't be a good idea to touch her lips today. Well, the woman thought she knew better and when she went to touch my horse's face, the animal quickly grabbed hold of the woman's center button on her sweater. My horse was trying desperately to yank the fastener off the woman just as desperately as the woman was attempting to keep her clothes on. I hopped off my mount, stuck my fingers her mouth (the horse's) and got her to loosen her grip on the woman's garment. The female was unharmed and quite amused at what had just occurred. She then went and put her fingers in my horse's mouth, as she'd seen me do in order to get her free. Well, you guessed it, my horse grabbed her fingers and wouldn't let go. I had to again get off my mount and repeat my previous performance. She was uninjured. I then asked the woman, "Please step back away from the horse. Please get away from the horse." Then I quickly rode as far away from her as I could, while still staying within my patrol area. Some people just don't listen.

We had a serious accident involving a pick-up truck with a lot of damage, but no driver around. We knew the driver was injured because there was a lot of blood and the windshield was smashed out. Unable to locate the driver, a tow truck was called and it lifted the front of the pick up off the ground in order to tow it away. It's then that we saw an arm come out from underneath the engine compartment. The man was dead at the scene. It appears that when the driver crashed into the utility pole, he went through the windshield. At the same time the hood buckled up and the driver went under the hood and into the engine compartment. The hood then slammed down after impact, concealing the driver inside.

As I pulled my cruiser up in front of the residence of a reported domestic call, I could see a young dark-haired man, in a pair of jeans and ripped T-shirt, leaning against the telephone pole. His head was bowed, with his left hand shielding his eyes and his right hand laying limp next to his side. He didn't move as I approached with obvious caution. I asked if he was the husband and he nodded yes without looking up. "So, what happened?" I inquired. Shaking his head slowly, he responded, "Officer, I just snapped. I was tired of coming home every single night and finding my wife in bed with my uncle."

A couple of vandals at a local ski resort decided to remove the foam pads which were used as protection for skiers who might otherwise accidentally ski into the base of the lift towers. One of the men died as a result of riding down the mountain on the foam pad he'd removed, and smashing into the same exact tower that he'd stolen the padding from. Talk about what goes around comes around.

Amateur hunters come up here during deer hunting season and cause all kinds of problem for the local residents. Unfortunately, they also cause death. A young woman who had heard something outside her house threw on a coat and white mittens before going outside to investigate. She saw a hunter and waved her arms, yelling for him to get off her property. The hunter shot and killed the woman on the spot. His lame excuse was that he thought the woman was a deer. All he saw were two white paws, so he shot.

A construction worker went to the emergency room and asked the nurse if she could help him out. A friend of his had jokingly pointed an electric nail gun at him and it went off, striking him. The nurse inquired as to where the nail had hit him and the man calmly removed his baseball cap. Sticking out of his head was a nail. Amazingly, it had missed by fractions of an inch any vital piece of brain tissue. He completely recovered and no charges were filed against his friend.

When we arrived at the scene of a two-car accident where neither vehicle could be driven further, we were informed that the driver of the car which had caused the accident had scurried down the sidewalk and into an office building. The woman was now headed back in our direction. My partner approached her and asked why she'd abruptly left the scene of the accident, especially since she was quite obviously injured in the collision. She said that she had to go and pay her insurance premium. She then fainted and we put her in an ambulance.

A car full of juveniles (16- and 17-year-olds), was driving erratically down the road. They noticed the cruiser and immediately pulled into the hospital parking lot near the emergency room entrance. By the time I got inside they were at the desk, as they lamely explained, to get a physical for a job they each were supposedly applying for the next day. After checking their licenses, I found that two of them had outstanding warrants, and that's why they were trying to avoid me.

A man trying to get himself a free soda out of a vending machine died in the attempt. He tried to loosen a soda by banging and tipping the apparatus. He ended up having the machine fall on top of him, crushing him to death. The victim caused his own demise.

I was dispatched to the scene of an accident and had my lights and siren on as I rounded the turn. The last thing I remember seeing was the ambulance as it impacted on the driver's side of the cruiser. The next thing I remember is waking up in the hospital in pain. I was later told that at the scene of my accident, in a part of the city known for drug activity, not one person came to help the ambulance personnel or myself. The people were gathering around the scene, chanting for one of the derelicts to get my gun. Fortunately, my fellow officers arrived and handled the situation before it'd gotten out of hand. It really does put into perspective the caliber of those individuals in that part of the city.

As I was driving down the highway, I noticed a woman stuck in the mud where she'd tried to make her own exit off the thruway. She said she'd missed the previous exit and had wanted to get to the sale at the store she'd seen from the highway. Instead of waiting for the next off ramp, she made her own exit and had gotten her Mercedes stuck up to the door in wet sod. I had to call a tow truck in order for her to be removed from the state property. While waiting for the tow truck she asked if she could go to the store and have me page her there when the truck showed up. I suggested that she wait right next to her vehicle for the tow truck. Amazing.

The careless woman left her two small children, aged three and five, in the car at a local mall while she went in "just for a minute." Well, she had left her keys in the ignition so the kids could listen to their children's story on cassette. The car smashed into four other parked cars before hitting the side of the brick building. The children both ended up in serious condition at the hospital, as a result. It appears that the five-year old hopped into the driver's seat and turned the key, starting the engine. He had to stand on his tip toes to reach the gas pedal and was barely able to hold onto the steering wheel. When they had hit the first vehicle or two, items from the seat fell onto the gas pedal which caused the boys foot to get caught and the car accelerated even more. It took us over twenty minutes to find the mother of the children who had only gone into the store for "just a minute."

The veteran motorcyclist later was able to recount to us, from his hospital bed, how he ended up smashing into the mail box and hedges on a local street. He always worn his helmet, glasses, leather gloves and jacket whenever he went for a ride, which definitely prevented him from sustaining more serious injuries. He had been driving the speed limit, which a number of witnesses can attest to, when he just veered into the stationary objects. He said he was taken off guard because he had just been stung in the ear, by a bee of some sort, which had gotten caught in between his helmet and head. During that split second that he had taken his eyes off the road and tried to determine what had stung him, it was too late and he crashed.

We were dispatched to a hit and run accident late one night on a two lane roadway on the outskirts of town. The man was dead at the scene and there were no skid marks to indicate that whoever had smashed into the unfortunate individual did not even attempt to stop before impact. We had little physical evidence at the scene of the accident to indicate what make and model of car or truck we would need to look for in order to start an immediate search for the killer. The forensics team worked at the scene well into the early dawn hours. Around 5:30 in the morning we received a call from a neighborhood resident regarding a car that had been vandalized during the night and had paint splattered on the hood of the car, as well as substantial damage done by a baseball bat or tire iron. They decided to call the police before waking the resident at that time of the morning. When we arrived at the address, we could see that it was not a case of vandalism but the auto that had killed the pedestrian earlier the previous night. When we rang the doorbell, a rather disheveled and still inebriated man answered the door. We asked him about the damage to his vehicle parked out front and inquired about his whereabouts the prior evening. He said he had a night out with the boys when a deer ran across the road in front of him on his way home. He had hit the deer but was too tired to stop and see if it was all right. That's probable how the car got damaged, he said, and he would call his insurance company later that morning to report the accident. We then informed him that it was not a deer that he had hit but a person, and the call he should be making was to a good attorney.

SOUNDING BOARD

This chapter covers different views and comments which the officers had expressed during the interviews and discussions I had with them. There was no specific topic relating to this chapter or its responses. I just kept taking notes and these are some of the comments they made.

The officers really do believe they get a "bad rap" from the public and the media alike. They don't receive the support from the communities they've been sworn to protect. There is also an enormous amount of frustration directed towards the prison system, as well as the courts. The officers do their jobs, arrest the criminals, and before they even finish the paperwork, the criminals are back out on the streets committing the same crimes or other crimes.

The comments are in no particular order. Just relax and read what the officers had to say when they were able to express their opinions.

As a regular law-abiding citizen, you have no rights until you break the law. Then you have all the rights in the world.

Many people think that the police profession in general is a simplistic vocation which doesn't require a great deal of aptitude. In reality, a police officer is required to have a mastery of more disciplines than perhaps any other occupation that exists. Many other people have a support staff and the luxury of time in their decision-making process, but the officer must process the information and make the decision right then and there. Without the luxury of time.

People fail to recognize humans make mistakes. We, as police officers, are still, to the best of my knowledge, considered as part of the human race. We have feelings, too. You need to respect the fact that it's a job. Off duty, I'm off duty. I'm far from perfect.

Affirmative Action has had a serious effect on the police departments. We no longer hire and promote based on knowledge and experience. It's done on quotas. There are a lot of good men and women that are more than qualified to do more than just a patrolman's job, but politics keep them from excelling. You can see it in their attitudes. It's so disheartening.

The public thinks that we're donut-eating, coffee-drinking, out-of-shape police officers. Incidentally, I eat Twinkies so I don't get crumbs on my uniform.

People automatically think that we're crooked or dishonest. They think we personally have something to gain by giving them a ticket. The people believe that it's like, "Gee, if I write two more tickets I can win a free microwave or three more and I can win a trip to the Bahamas." It's ridiculous.

People get amnesia. They forget the fact that we're there to enforce the law. They forget that we're there to help them.

Just because you put your flashers on when double-parked doesn't make it right. In fact, you are admitting you're in the wrong. Otherwise you wouldn't have put your lights on. Don't double park.

Sometimes I honestly believe that abortion should be retroactive.

Defense attorneys that represent drug dealers should have a way that they have to account for the money they received from their client—the drug dealer that has no real job and no visible means of income except dealing drugs. There should be full disclosure. No more "brown paper bag transactions."

We're probably the only profession that gets assaulted on a daily basis just because of the profession we've chosen.

Our court system has failed dramatically. There's no question about it.

95% of those we arrest deserve to be arrested. If there's a mistake in a procedure then it punishes the public as well. Letting a criminal off because a box wasn't properly checked off on a report is a travesty.

When people have to keep several guns in their home to protect their own property, they have become prisoners in that very same home.

They expect us to solve all their problems. We're not psychiatric doctors, although I feel like it sometimes.

Sometimes while working undercover in narcotics, we need to obtain a "suppressed license" which is an alternate license we use for identification, issued to law enforcement personnel in a fictitious name by the state. When I received mine, I should have checked on the name, first. I had mistakenly used the name of a real felon who was wanted by another law enforcement agency. It did cause more than a few problems for me a few months down the road.

Sometimes when you try to do a good deed for a person, you end up feeling like you got a kick in the teeth. I noticed a woman drive by with her coat dragging on the ground. I pulled her over and proceeded to let her know that her coat was hanging out her door. She started to yell at me and tell me that I scared her half to death by pulling her over and that she was going to report me to my supervisor for stopping her without just cause. She was belligerent. I counted to ten silently to myself, wished her a better day and went back to my cruiser. Sometimes you just can't do things right by people. Oh, well.

Crime is everyone's problem. Without the public getting involved, there will always be crimes and criminals getting away with it.

The general public sees the uniform and not the face or personality. We are non-people, void of individual characteristics.

Public contact is negative. They only call when they have a problem. People have a warped perception of the way the laws are. Then, if you tell them something they don't want to hear, they get mad at you.

Human life becomes important once the pressure groups get involved along with the State. There is so much liberalism. When drugs were just a city problem, the penalties were stiffer. Once they made their way into the suburbs, drug offenses became decriminalized from a felony to a misdemeanor.

The police department is quasi-military. There is a chain of command. We have rules and regulations.

I have a rule: anyone I pull over for a violation that starts the conversation with, "Don't you have anything else better to do?" always gets a ticket. It usually is more than one, because there's almost always something else either wrong with their auto or another violation that I might have overlooked earlier.

Most people think that all white cops are bad. Racism. When people call us for assistance, they have attitudes as soon as we arrive. They called us; we didn't call them. We're here to help them with their complaint and when we start asking questions, they think we're harassing them. We don't treat anyone any different from the next.

———

There is no respect like there was in the past for law enforcement officers. If we're not to a call immediately, they get upset and start yelling at us.

———

Blame: never blame the person who did the crime. Find a government agency or someone with big shoulders to put the blame on. It's the constant "Not me; not my fault" syndrome.

———

Frequently when I stop someone for speeding they will complain about the other motorists speeding by while I'm writing their ticket. "Look at that guy, he's speeding. Why don't you go get him instead of me?" Usually I try to ignore them. Sometimes it's difficult. On a few occasions I've been a little sardonic. For instance, I'd ask them if they'd ever gone fishing? (Yes.) Did you catch every fish in the river? (No.) "Neither do I, but I keep trying!" That usually gets them to be quiet. Although I had one guy in court tell the judge that all I wanted to talk about after I'd caught him was "fishing."

———

One muggy summer evening we had to do a search warrant which later led to the arrest of the individual in a housing project. In one of the rooms, the wall looked like it was moving. I blinked a few times and found that in a way, it *was* moving. There were so many bugs crawling on the wall that it almost looked like wall paper. I hate doing these searches.

———

Post Traumatic Stress Behavior is very real. The debriefing of the officers after a traumatic incident really needs to be addressed.

_____

Most criminals are less than animals. Animals at least protect their young. These creatures don't. They'll sacrifice their wives, girlfriends and many times their children.

_____

If you aren't part of the solution (to stop crime) then you're part of the problem.

_____

Why do people always have to blame me when I give them a ticket for speeding? They tell me it'll be my fault if they lose their license. As if I was the one that made them speed. People: grow up and get a life! Take responsibility for your actions.

_____

It used to be fun to be an officer. I enjoyed helping people. But what I need to do most is make sure that I cover my butt. Keep at an arms distance from everyone, because you never know who will bring you up on false charges of a racial or sexual nature, or police brutality. The courts have left it wide open for anybody to sue anybody. If I have to use force against the criminals on the street that frequently carry automatic weapons, I'll be held accountable if I need to protect myself. These scumbags even wear bullet proof vests, yet when we arrest them for a crime, they claim they weren't doing anything wrong. Wake up public! Why are they wearing bullet proof vests if they are innocent of any crime?

_____

The excuses are always the same during morning rush hour: "I'm late for work." During the evening rush hour, they're ". . . anxious to get home."

_____

People need to be more responsible in the upbringing of their children. Children learn by example. If you do drugs, they'll do drugs. If you hit your spouse, they'll think it's acceptable to hit their's when they get married.

_____

No one ever takes responsibility for their actions. They blame everyone else for their problems. It's society's fault they don't work. Of course they've never gotten up before noon or even applied for a job. It's society's fault because they are on drugs. If they took a minute to look in a mirror instead of using it to snort cocaine up their noses, they'd see that it is their reflection in the mirror and not society's. They are responsible for their life and the shambles they've made of it. But that's O.K. We as tax payers will supply them with food stamps, welfare and a place to live, all without lifting a finger. Society is only responsible for being an enabler to the lazy, pathetic excuse for a human being.

_____

Don't let your kid become a cop. And if he wants to be a lawyer—shoot him!

COMMENTARY

Author's note: This section presents commentaries written by several different people covering a variety of topics.

Frustration .... **page 110**
> by an anonymous Police Officer

Me, The Lousy Cop .... **page 114**
> author unknown (received via-e-mail)

Code 2 .... **page 116**
> by Lieutenant Michael Manzi, Hartford, Connecticut Police Department

Let's Make it Personal .... **page 118**
> by Linda Kleinschmidt

Commentary

FRUSTRATION
by an anonymous Police Officer

(Reprinted in its entirety from **Police on Patrol: The Other Side of the Story**)

My frustration is now complete. Never did I dream I would encounter such obstacles as I have faced in the past years of police work. The obstacles I expected were to originate from the "bad guys." The largest and most stress producing obstacles I faced never pointed a gun at me or threatened to do me physical harm. If someone had told me the toughest battles would be fought within the four walls of the police department, I would have shrugged it off as a "sour grapes" comment from a cynical individual ready to retire. I have learned, first hand, there is more stress produced by those "on our side" then I ever faced on the street.

There are considerable differences between those who are employed in the private sectors as managers and those who are "managers" within an area of government whether it is at the federal level or the municipal level. The differences are noticeable. Private sector managers (CEO's, presidents, department heads, etc.) are aware that new and creative ideas are absolutely necessary in order to stay in business and ahead of the competition. They realize that saving money is the same as earning it. They are aware that an efficient operation is also an effective one. These concepts are incorporated within company philosophies because they know that they do not have the luxury of the bottomless pocketbook called the taxpayer to fund their business. Change is necessary. Progressive attitudes are a must. Attacking age-old problems with new ideas is welcome. Government managers have a different slant when it applies to progressive attitudes. Change is challenged more vehemently by government administrators as it is perceived as failure on their part, unless of course, it enlarges their own bureaucracy. But bureaucracies do not fight crime. The working cop on the street has to fight the criminals and the bureaucrats. And guess which one is the worst foe of the two?

Administrators who fight change and progressive tactics all have the battle cry "that's the way we did it twenty years ago" or "this has been working for the past ten years; why change now?" I do not have the statistics to support the next statement but I believe that those who attain management levels in the private sector and then join a government agency bring with them the positive attitudes and progressive thinking and eventually become assets to their agencies by looking further than the end of the

110

fiscal year. Government employees, on the other hand, that make the jump to the private sector bring with them outdated, antiquated attitudes that are so prevalent among bureaucracies. This type of short-sighted behavior has to be eliminated if government wishes to attain more with their current budgets. Anyone handling a multi-million dollar budget has to be aware of their investments and the potential returns for a period greater than one fiscal year. Only within a government agency could ineffectiveness and inefficiency be rewarded. Only a branch of government would boast about its short-sighted, narrow-minded and self-serving efforts. An individual of vision who can attack an old problem in a new and creative fashion need not apply. Those who present fresh ideas are considered wave-makers and boat-rockers. Pass out the life vests I say.

All through your career you will be told you need to be a team player. Their definition of team goes something like this. You are on your way to being a team player if:

1. They like you.
   The hell with your work record, work ethic or character. "He can't write a report to save his life and has a pattern of excessive sick time but he's a hell of a guy and doesn't get under my skin."

2. You are not the subject of any controversy where the administration may be questioned about your actions or decisions.

   Police work is fraught with controversy. A good cop, a cop doing the job he was hired to do, will be controversial. Period. That's just the way it is. Supreme Court decisions arise from cops doing their job.

3. You agree with their (the administration or a specific administrator's) philosophies and politics.

Lord forbid you should disagree with either of these. One of the reasons they attain their present position has to do with politics. These people will pander to the politically correct crowd and expect you to do the same. A flip-flop of policy is the norm. They tend to do what is popular rather than what is right for all concerned.

The real killer is when they use the condescending phrase "there is no "I" in 'T-E-A-M'." I see a lot of "I's" in "TEAM." A team is made up of *individuals* with a common goal or purpose. Each individual brings certain characteristics, talents and abilities to the team. *Initiative* is a positive and much sought after characteristic necessary for team work. A person with an *industrious* nature is an asset. The biggest "I," the most important "I" that seems to be overlooked, is *integrity*. Without integrity you are nothing. Your team is nothing. Personal integrity, honesty and the refusal to compromise is never considered (unless of course, they don't like you) you are controversial or you are not in lock-step with their politics. But then again, someone who changes their beliefs in order to be politically correct can't have much in the way of integrity.

Moving outside the four walls and into the state legislature, one can view the most transparent of all people: our lawmakers. Lawyers making laws. Does that seem like a conflict of interest to anybody? Built-in loopholes made by practicing attorneys. Laws so convoluted and overly complicated that successful prosecution is nearly impossible. Keep in mind that most lawyers are not involved in courtroom drama everyday as seen on "LA Law" or "Matlock" or other attorney-based television shows. An attorney contends with lots and lots of routine, mundane, monotonous paperwork everyday. They become accustomed to an overabundance of paperwork and sometimes cannot function unless there is a mountain of forms to accompany their daily routine. So it seems natural it would carry over when creating or revising laws. Then again, many of us wonder if the extensive paperwork is created just on the chance that the working cop, after a busy shift, may forget to fill in an area or check off a box on a report, thus making the arrest null. Who knows?

Our law makers are politicians first and foremost. They will create new laws and revise old laws to make them "tougher" based on the public opinion at the time. The public wants tougher laws? We'll make the tougher laws so be sure to vote for us the next time because we did what you wanted. Common sense apparently has no role when the legislature is in session. For example, anyone caught in possession of or selling drugs within fifteen feet of a school, housing project or state-licensed and approved day care center (town approved doesn't count) is subjected to stiffer penalties than the regular drug dealer on any other street. I can stand at the school bus stop and sell drugs or stop the mothers as they bring their kids to day care and sell them drugs, and as long as I am more than fifteen hundred feet away from a school, housing project or day care center, I will not be subject to as severe a penalty. Hell, I can ride the school bus and sell drugs to each child entering the bus and still will not serve as stiff a sentence if I get caught, as long as *I am not within fifteen hundred feet of a school, housing project, or state-certified day care center.* According to our lawmakers, those residing in housing projects require more protection than the rest of the community. Children attending city or town certified day care centers are not protected with the same tenacity as those who attend state-certified centers. How is that for a law that creates second-class citizens? It seems as though our law makers have decided that those dealing drugs to children are bad only if they are near a specific area. The others dealing drugs to children aren't so bad, for some foolish reason only our State Representatives and Senators can comprehend.

The lawmakers cannot shoulder all the blame for our ineffective criminal justice system. The courts have lent a hand in making it impossible to keep the worst of society off the streets, too. The United States Supreme Court recently adopted what is referred to as a "plain feel doctrine" (Minnesota vs. Dickerson). When an officer conducts a pat down of the outer clothing of an individual, he is feeling for a weapon or something that may be used as a weapon. Many times during the pat down, the officer through his training and experience, can determine by touch that an object secreted in a pocket is in fact some form of narcotics. When the officer feels the object and can conclude it is narcotics, the common sense approach is to remove the item from the pocket and examine it. The "plain feel" part comes from the fact that an officer, by touch, can distinguish a weapon from the other items they commonly carried in a pocket because it does not feel like a weapon. Has Connecticut adopted this common sense doctrine? You guessed it! An appellate court has ruled that the removal of narcotics from an individual after this has been identified by touch, is an illegal search and the evidence must therefore be suppressed. Let's hope the Connecticut Supreme Court rules otherwise.

Most of us can face the bad guys no matter what they throw in our direction but we can't fight our battles on three fronts. It's not the bad guys that beat us down, it is the police administrators who constantly and consistently demonstrate regressive attitudes and refuse to accept any form of change; it is the lawmakers making complicated, nearly unenforceable laws, and when they are enforceable, prosecution is limited at best. And last, the liberal courts worry more about the rights of the accused rather than the rights of the individual or the community. I would like to bring our lawmakers and judges to see the battered, broken and bloody body of an infant who received fatal injuries from its crack-smoking father who couldn't stand the child's constant crying and decided to swing it around by its feet and dash its head against the floor until the child died, and see what they would have to say about the accused's rights.

Me, The Lousy Cop
Author Unknown

Well, Mr. Citizen, I guess you've got me figured out. I seem to fit neatly into the category you placed me in. I'm stereotyped, characterized, classified, grouped and always typical. I'm the Lousy Cop.

Unfortunately, the reverse isn't true. I can never figure you out.

From birth you teach your children that I'm a bogeyman and they are shocked when they learn and identify me with my traditional enemy, the criminal.

You can raise Cain about the guy who cuts you off in traffic, but let me catch you doing the same thing and it's picking on you. You know all the traffic laws, but you never got the single ticket you deserved.

You accuse me of coddling juveniles until I catch your kid doing something. Then it's "badge happy."

You take an hour lunch and several coffee breaks each day but point me out as a loafer if you see me having just one cup.

You pride yourself on your polished manners but think nothing of interrupting my meal at noon with your troubles.

You shout "foul" if you observe me driving en route to an emergency call, but raise hell if I take more than 10 seconds responding to your call.

You're a witty conversationalist, but bore me stiff at social gatherings with your vast knowledge of law enforcement

You call it "part of my job" if someone strikes me, but it's police brutality if I strike back.

You wouldn't think of telling your dentist how to pull a decayed tooth, or your doctor how to take out your appendix, but you are always willing to give me a few pointers on law enforcement.

You talk to me in a manner (and use language) that would assure a bloody nose from anybody else, but you expect me to stand and take it without batting an eye.

You cry "Something has to be done about all this crime," but, of course, you can't be bothered with getting involved.

And what about the guy that works all night making sure you didn't forget to lock up your business or home when you left on vacation?

You've got no use for me at all, but of course, it's okay if I change a tire for your wife, or deliver your child in the back seat of my patrol car on the way to the hospital, save your son's life with mouth-to-mouth resuscitation, or maybe work many hours overtime to find your lost daughter.

So, Mr. Citizen, you stand there on your soap box, and rant and rave about the way I do my job, calling me every name in the book, but never stop for a minute to think that your property, your family or maybe your life might depend on one thing, me or one of my buddies.

Yes, Mr. Citizen, me . . . the lousy cop.

CODE 2
by Lieutenant Michael Manzi (18 year veteran)

Nationally, there has been considerable public debate involving police pursuits. The heightened interest may have been promulgated by the Fox network televising such specials as "The World's Scariest Police Chases." Anyhow, many political leaders have challenged police departments throughout the country on their policy as to when officers may or may not engage in pursuit of criminal offenders. Two political leaders in Connecticut have attempted to spearhead a legislative session which would attempt to revise existing policy in regard to police pursuits. They stressed that officers should be better trained. One of these leaders (names purposely omitted) even suggested that criminal offenders engaging officers in pursuit would have an additional 10 days added to their sentence. Isn't that marvelous.

Unequivocally, the arguable factor and concern of these politicians is for the safety of innocent parties. All reasonable people will agree that no innocent person should ever have to cross the path of a fleeing felon. Every officer on the street understands that safety is of the utmost importance when he engages in pursuit of a fleeing vehicle. However, police officers are now in a Catch-22 situation. Should the serious criminal offender be allowed to slip back into society simply by driving away from the officer?

The Hartford, Connecticut Police Department has a Policy and Procedure Order governing police pursuits. Article III, Sec. A clearly states: "Police pursuits are a serious matter with the potential for property damage, personal injury and death." Further, there are 28 different variables that the officer has to consider while engaging in pursuit of a fleeing vehicle. There is periodic roll call training in regard to this order and all officers are advised of the vicarious liability involved in police pursuits. Each pursuit in the City of Hartford is reviewed and evaluated by a Commander to ensure compliance with the Policy and Procedure Order. Chases are often discussed between supervisors and officers for additional training purposes.

Lawmakers can calmly sit in their offices on Monday morning and criticize and evaluate police pursuits. However, there is one element they rarely consider. That is, the adrenaline that rushes through the police officer when he throws the overhead lights on and activates the siren. Often times the officer encounters the "tunnel vision" effect when he is in pursuit of a vehicle which has just involved a shooting incident. This is a human reaction to an extremely stressful situation. At this very time, the officer must understand that the apprehension of the criminal offender should not outweigh the safety of all the parties involved. Officers are cognizant of the fact they do not chase criminal offenders in school zones, the wrong way on highways, or into congested areas, no matter what the crime was. Supervisors carefully monitor all chases and more often than not call them off when the pursuit reaches a level that would justify an extreme indifference to human life.

Over the past few years it has become easy to point the finger and blame the police. However, that accusatory finger should be pointed in the direction of the criminal offender. Legislators should impose serious time for criminal offenders who engage police in pursuit. Presently, the Connecticut Motor Vehicle Law, 14-223 (b), "Engaging Police in Pursuit," is punishable by a misdemeanor motor vehicle summons for the first offense. A mandatory one-year jail sentence would be appropriate for the criminal offenders engaging police in pursuit, providing the initial offense committed was a felony. After all, innocent people should not be hurt because of the reckless abandonment of the criminal offender.

LET'S MAKE IT PERSONAL
by Linda Kleinschmidt

After interviewing literally hundreds of law enforcement personnel during the past four years, it has become evident that the lack of follow-through by the judicial system has greatly diminished the effectiveness of these fine individuals. They risk their lives with dangerous criminals in order to protect the citizens of these United States. Yet when they need to use force against those who wish to harm or destroy the lives of innocent citizens, their actions are put on trial under a microscope by the media. Important facts which can't be publicly disclosed during an on-going investigation are then speculated on by the media and judged before the public on TV, radio and newsprint. The criminal is almost always portrayed as the unfortunate individual done an injustice by the badge-carrying officer. Not only that, but the first accusation made by the press is "racism" in cases where the criminal is of minority background.

The public isn't made privy to prior arrests—which in most cases are numerous—of the individual who was caught breaking the law. The officer may be someone who has comforted those in times of anguish and accidents, and saved the lives of other individuals, but once the press gets involved, the officer is the villain when the criminal gets hurt or dies. The media will flash pathetic pictures on the screen repeatedly to induce sympathy and anger at what the officer has done in obviously abusing the "poor criminal." Yet, do we see the bandages and the bruises they had inflicted on the officer? *No!* We see a picture of the officer in full uniform in a posed portrait taken for another occasion.

Why do we constantly inflict upon these sworn officers a double-edged sword of damned-if-they-do and damned-if-they-don't. Most, if not all, hiring of law enforcement personnel undergoes extensive scrutiny to insure the proper attitude and aptitude of a potential law enforcement candidate. Yet the media and lay people pass judgment on these individuals without the officers being able to vindicate themselves when publicly accused and scorned.

It's about time we stopped making uninformed opinions and judgments of the officers without all the facts. One sure "fact" is that the media has not done their homework and has not or is unable to give information which would allow us to make informed decisions. That is actually the job of the failing judicial system.

We cannot count on the courts to administer justice because it is not a court of justice but a court of law. Even then the laws and interpretation of the laws have been turned and twisted so much in favor of the criminal that it's akin to a pretzel.

We need to make those who break our laws accountable for their actions. Plea bargaining should only be used in extreme cases and only once in a lifetime for the criminal. We should also let the judges and attorneys know that we want them to make sure those individuals who broke the law will not just become a number. Their full and often extensive criminal history should be made public along with the actual time served—if any—for prior convictions.

We should no longer tolerate these parasites and leeches of modern society. Their prison terms should be what was imposed on them: five years = five years. Not one or two years with time off for so called "good behavior." The victims they create by their criminal actions are not getting time off. Just think of the court time which will be saved because these repeat offenders will not be out on the streets committing more crimes. It will send a message of zero tolerance to the drug community of their illegal actions. Also, here in Connecticut, they should only be allowed three continuances in court instead of eight.

We offer them education within the prisons, so that when they come out they are able to work. They could then become part of society, instead of separate. The argument of "having a bad life" (and that's why they committed their crimes) could no longer hold up because the negative influences of drugs and violence would have a zero tolerance. Young impressionable children could see what would happen if they turned their lives to crime. Gone would be the glamour, or as they refer to it the "respect"—the ability to accumulate money through illegal operations and flaunt it in front of young children and teenagers.

We have the tools to accomplish this. We just need to be firm and committed to making a difference. The prisons would not be overcrowded because the actual numbers would only fluctuate with "newer" convicts and not repeat offenders. Not everyone will stop dealing drugs, but a large dent could be made.

Access to illegal drugs within the walls of the prison would decrease once adequate measures are taken to insure that corruptible correction officers were not allowed to walk freely into and out of the prisons. A viable suggestion would be for State Troopers to scan items and all persons going into the correction facilities. The canine division of the State Police could be brought to each facility every day for approximately two weeks. This way you could watch the prisoners and see which ones are having severe drug withdrawal systems. This would also enable the correction department to better focus on the people who have direct contact with these inmates and be able to apprehend those who are bringing in the drugs. There are solutions; you only have to take a step back and look. You have to put the politics aside and do the job of assuring drug-free jails and honest correction officers.

The temptation and accessibility of bringing in contraband to influential inmates is always a potential risk. Until the problem of drugs within the correction system is eliminated, a "we trust our employees" attitude by Corrections needs to be changed. Drugs are in the hands of those who have demonstrated they have no regard for the laws; that's why they're in jail.

The inmates gave up their constitutional rights once they broke the law. We should start making prisons a place where no one would want to be. If we do this and be firm, a number of individuals will not repeat their past activities and possibly become productive citizens. We have a long way to go, but as with everything worth something, it starts with a step forward.

We need to make it personal.

THE PERMAMENT TRIBUTE

I felt it was important to include in this book information about Connecticut's Law Enforcement Memorial, a Permanent Tribute to those here in Connecticut that have lost their lives in the line of duty. This memorial was the first state memorial of its kind in the country.

For those of you reading this, who don't already have a memorial for those within your state that lost their lives, this may be a great idea to copy. The men and women in blue that serve your state would be proud that you've decided to always honor and remember those who served, protected and paid the ultimate price: the loss of their lives.

The following is reprinted with the permission of those in charge of the Memorial Foundation.

> The Memorial Project was born out of a ceremony at the Groton Long Point Police Department in May 1985. Long Point Chief Al Burbank was responsible for the first statewide law enforcement memorial services for the officers who had been killed in the line of duty.
>
> Chief Tom Rotunda of the Ridgefield Police Department, president of the Connecticut Police Chiefs Association at that time, was quite moved by

the memorial service and decided to take some action to ensure that a permanent memorial would be erected for officers at the federal, state and local levels who had lost their lives while serving the citizens of Connecticut.

Under the direction of Chief Rotunda, the Connecticut Police Chiefs Association undertook what became a multi-year project in an effort to construct the first state Police Memorial in the country. A committee was formed consisting of individuals from all aspects of the law enforcement community, business people, and other citizens who had an interest in working on this project.

In June 1985, the committee began to choose a design for the Memorial. The winning design was submitted by architect Jonathan Humble.

In February 1986, the committee chose to erect the memorial at the Connecticut Police Academy in Meriden. This site was chosen primarily because of the impact upon both recruits and veteran officers who use these facilities.

Funds to build the memorial were raised during the next several years. Mr. Tom Sarubbi, who was an executive vice-president of Sentinel Bank in Hartford, undertook the difficult job of Finance Chairman. Through his efforts and that of several Chiefs throughout Connecticut, fund-raising activities were held and donations sought from individuals and corporations. It took several years to raise the approximately $375,000 necessary to construct the memorial.

The job of erecting the memorial was given to Geno J. Lupinacci, who specializes in memorial projects. Jaime Almeda of Associated Construction in Hartford agreed to oversee the construction of the project. In the summer of 1989, the first pieces of granite began to arrive at the building site. It took approximately two months to construct the memorial.

The memorial contains the names of fallen officers from federal agencies, including the FBI and Customs, the Connecticut State Police Department and many municipal departments throughout the State of Connecticut.

The Connecticut Law Enforcement Memorial is a constant reminder of the difficult tasks officers face, and the ultimate sacrifice that they may be called upon to make.

On behalf of the Connecticut Police Chiefs Association and the entire Connecticut law enforcement community, we thank all the private individuals, family members of the deceased, and corporations for their efforts in erecting this permanent tribute to those officers who paid the ultimate price.

If you are interested in making a donation to the Memorial Foundation, please make your check out to CT Law Enforcement Memorial Foundation and mail to: 285 Preston Ave. Meriden, CT 06450.

ABOUT THE AUTHOR

Linda Kleinschmidt was born and raised in Connecticut, having grown up on a cattle ranch and tree farm that her family owns in a quiet country town.

Before she began researching and writing books about law enforcement, she worked in the advertising field doing sales as well as ad design and layout. She is the sole owner of AJ Publishing Company, named for her daughter Andrea Juliana.

Although she enjoys the work that delves her into the world of law enforcement, she has never had any desire to be a police officer. Her goal is to help the public understand . . . understand that what they see on television or read in the local newspapers is only a fraction of what the police actually do in order to protect us. She wants to provide awareness, education and most importantly, the *positive* side of law enforcement.